JUST ANOTHER TOOL...

REAL ESTATE CONTRACTS

TERRY L. WHITE

President & CEO Sunwest Escrow, LC

ISBN 9781541268173

Foreword

I have found that most individuals who want to buy or sell real estate have some knowledge about conventional loans, FHA loans, or VA loans, but few have knowledge about Real Estate Contracts. Real Estate Contracts can accomplish the same thing. As far as I'm concerned, Real Estate Contracts are just another tool in the tool box.

This book is presented as an informational guide to those of you who may have heard of Real Estate Contracts and want more information; to those of you who have an interest in Real Estate Contracts; and to those of you who are Real Estate Professionals and desire to be better informed regarding Real Estate Contracts.

As an informational guide for Real Estate Contract basics, this book is intended for a broad audience; and the laws and procedures presented herein pertain only to the state of New Mexico.

I wrote this book from an Escrow Agent's point of view; it is based upon my many years' experience in this industry. It is also based upon my continuing education class on this subject in which I present Real Estate Contracts as just another tool to be used in the buying and selling of real property.

Real Estate Contracts are not right for every situation, but in many situations they may be used effectively. My intention is to dispel any myths about Real Estate Contracts and to present information that shows they can be win/win situations for both parties, providing those parties are informed and counsel with their team of professionals.

I hope this book is helpful to you.

Terry L. White

President & CEO of Sunwest Escrow, LC

Table of Contents

INTRODUCTION

WHAT IS A REAL ESTATE CONTRACT?

In New Mexico, a Real Estate Contract is one of several different types of arrangements commonly referred to as owner-financing. Let's begin by defining what is meant by owner-financing, as the term is used in this book.

Generally speaking, owner-financing is used in connection with real estate sales to describe a private sale wherein the owner or individual who is selling the real property acts as the bank for the individual who wants to buy the real property.

In effect, the seller/owner lends the money to the buyer/borrower. The buyer/borrower makes payments, plus interest, to the seller/owner over the term of the loan until such time as the loan is repaid or the buyer/borrower defaults on the loan. The type of owner-financing arrangement used determines at what stage the buyer/borrower receives the deed to the property, and the remedies available to both parties in the case of default.

This book is intended to give a purely informational and anecdotal overview of Real Estate Contracts as governed by the state of New Mexico. The information contained in this book is not intended, nor should it be construed to give legal, accounting, tax, investment, or real estate advice. Before entering into any agreement concerning

the purchase, sale, or investment in real estate, individuals are urged to consult with their own team of licensed professionals.

CHAPTER 1

A REVIEW OF THE TOOLS USED IN BUYING AND SELLING REAL ESTATE

OWNER-FINANCING—JUST ANOTHER TOOL

In order to develop a proper perspective, one should think of owner-financing as just another tool that may be used to accomplish the objective of buying or selling real property.

Chances are that real estate professionals and non-professionals have heard of the terms conventional mortgage, FHA loan, and VA loan, and readily think of one of these terms when considering the purchase or sale of real estate. For real estate professionals, no doubt these terms are familiar. Since I want this book to be useful to professionals and non-professionals alike, allow me to give a brief overview of these terms and articulate the differences among them.

I will briefly describe these tools so that individuals may see where owner-financing fits into the *tool box* in the purchase or sale of real estate.

CONVENTIONAL LOAN

Conventional loans are offered by banks, savings and loans, credit unions, and mortgage companies. These institutions follow and apply federal guidelines covering credit scores, minimum down payments, and debt-to-income ratios to determine whether or not an individual may qualify for a conventional, conforming loan. Lenders generally like issuing conforming loans, since these loans may be sold to the governmental agencies of Fannie Mae and Freddie Mac; this means that the lender does not have to carry the loan or debt on its books.

Credit Score

In order to qualify for a conventional, conforming loan, a borrower is typically required to have good or excellent credit; the credit score determines the interest rate to be charged on the loan and the amount of the down payment required.

Debt to Income Ratio

In a conventional, conforming loan, the lender generally likes the borrower to have a low debt-to-income ratio; typically, the percentage that is desirable is 36% (Bankrate.com, Top 10 Mortgage Tips for Potential Buyers in 2016, updated December 31, 2015). This ratio looks at the total amount of the borrower's monthly consumer debt and compares it with the borrower's total amount of monthly gross income. This ratio is used to ascertain the borrower's ability to make monthly payments.

Down Payment

Generally, if a borrower makes a 20% down payment, there is no Private Mortgage Insurance (PMI) required. If the down payment is less than 20%, Private Mortgage Insurance is required.

Chapter 1

Mortgage Insurance

Private Mortgage Insurance is issued for the benefit of the lender, and not the borrower. In case the borrower is unable to make the mortgage payments, the Private Mortgage Insurance policy will pay a partial amount of the loan balance to the lender. This type of policy allows lenders to make conventional loans to individuals who may not have a 20% down payment.

The premium charged for the Private Mortgage Insurance is affected by the amount of the down payment and the borrower's credit score. Generally speaking, the lower the down payment and/or the lower the credit score, the higher the premium charged for the Private Mortgage Insurance.

Generally, the charge for Private Mortgage Insurance continues until such time as the loan-to-value ratio equals 78% of the original appraised value of the home. At that time, the lender generally cancels the Private Mortgage Insurance.

Size of the Loan

The federal guidelines which apply to conventional, conforming loans generally limit the size of the loan to $417,000.00 for a single-family dwelling; although certain counties in the different regional areas have higher conventional, conforming loan limits. There are higher limits if the property is more than a single-family dwelling, as well.

It is possible to obtain a higher loan amount than $417,000.00, and this is referred to as a non-conforming, jumbo loan. The non-conforming, jumbo loans generally require a higher interest rate and larger down payment.

Other

Conventional loans can be used for owner-occupied real estate or may be used to purchase investment properties. Investment properties generally require a higher interest rate on the loan and a larger down payment.

If there are items or issues with the property requiring repair, this does not impede the loan's approval process. It is the buyer and seller who work out the details of whom will make the repairs, and the repairs are generally completed before closing can occur.

Generally speaking, conventional mortgages are not *assumable*; this means that another individual is unable to take over the payments, yet keep the underlying mortgage.

FEDERAL HOUSING ADMINISTRATION (FHA) LOAN

The same banking and lending institutions which issue conventional, conforming loans, may also issue Federal Housing Administration (FHA) loans, if they are an FHA-approved lender. Note that FHA loans are government-insured loans, and not loans issued by the federal government.

Down Payment

An FHA loan allows individuals with lower credit scores to obtain a mortgage. In contrast to a conventional, conforming loan, the minimum down payment required for an FHA loan is 3.5% of the purchase price. If the borrower is at the lower end of the credit-score spectrum, one may have to pay a higher percentage of down payment in order to qualify.

Chapter 1

Relative to a lower position on the credit-score spectrum, the period of time that has elapsed since a foreclosure or a bankruptcy appeared on the borrower's credit report can be shorter with an FHA loan, than with a conventional, conforming loan.

Debt to Income

The total amount of the borrower's monthly consumer debt compared with the borrower's monthly gross income or the debt-to-income ratio can be as high as 43% with an FHA loan; and may be slightly higher depending on compensating factors (portal.hud.gov, Section F Borrowing Qualifying Ratios Overview).

Mortgage Insurance

With an FHA loan, two Mortgage Insurance Premiums (MIPs) are required. This is the way in which the government insures the loans for the lender. One of the Mortgage Insurance Premiums is an upfront mortgage insurance premium that is a stated percentage of the loan amount; it is due at closing.

The second Mortgage Insurance Premium is an annual premium that can be payable for most of the life of the mortgage. Its cost is a percentage of the loan amount and takes into account the term of the loan, as well as the loan-to-value ratio at the time the loan was originated.

The loan-to-value ratio at origination measures the amount of the loan against the total value of the property; hence, this ratio is impacted by the amount of the down payment. The higher the down payment is, the lower the loan-to-value ratio; and the lower the down payment, the higher the loan-to-value ratio. Higher loan-to-value ratios may require higher premiums; in addition, these premiums could be paid for the entire term of the mortgage.

Size

The amount that may be financed under an FHA loan is regulated and contingent on the county wherein the borrower is purchasing the property, as well as whether or not the property is more than a single-family dwelling.

Other

Unlike conventional, conforming loans, FHA loans are only available for owner-occupied real estate; they are not available for investment property. Further, the lender may require that certain repairs be made to the property before the loan is approved; this ensures the property conforms to FHA minimum property standards.

Although there may be restrictions on an FHA loan, note that FHA loans are generally *assumable* with qualification; this means that the payments under an original FHA loan may be taken over by another qualified borrower.

VETERANS AFFAIRS (VA) LOANS

The same banking and lending institutions that issue conventional, conforming loans, and/or FHA loans, may also issue Veterans Affairs (VA) loans, providing they are a VA-approved lender. As with the FHA loans, VA loans are government-insured loans, and not loans issued by the federal government or a federal agency. Since the loan is guaranteed by the federal government, this means the lending institution assumes less risk.

As the name implies, VA loans restrict who may apply for these loans to active-duty military personnel or veterans, and

Chapter 1

some, select surviving spouses (providing they have not remarried). The amount that may be financed under a VA loan is regulated and contingent on the county wherein the borrower is purchasing the property, as well as whether or not the property is more than a single-family dwelling.

Down Payment

VA loans permit 100% financing; this means that the borrower is not required to make a down payment. With a VA loan, the lender will allow the borrower to have a debt-to-income ratio of up to 41% (freddiemac.com, Department of Veterans Affairs VA Mortgage). In addition, unlike conventional, conforming loans, and/or FHA loans however, the borrower with a VA loan is not required to make mortgage insurance premiums (PMI or MIP).

Funding Fee

In lieu of mortgage insurance premiums, the borrower is required to pay a "funding fee" at closing. This funding fee is a percentage of the loan amount, contingent on whether or not the borrower made a down payment, and whether the borrower is using the VA benefit for the first time or for a subsequent time. The funding fee is applied to ensure that the VA loan program will continue to be available to qualified military personnel.

Other

Like the FHA loan, VA loans are available only for owner-occupied real estate; they are not available for investment property. Further, the lender may require that certain repairs be made to the property before the loan is approved, to ensure that it conforms to VA minimum property standards

VA loans may carry restrictions, but like the FHA loans, these VA loans are generally *assumable* with qualification; and payments may be taken over by another qualified borrower. By qualified borrower, this means either a military person or a non-military person.

If the individual who assumes the loan is a non-military person, the VA entitlement stays with the property on which the mortgage is assumed. This means the original VA borrower could not use the VA entitlement on another property.

FINAL NOTE ON THESE COMMON LOAN TYPES

The Federal Housing Finance Authority (FHFA) sets the standards to which Conventional loans must conform to enable lenders the ability to sell their mortgages to Fannie Mae and Freddie Mac. The U. S. Department for Housing and Urban Development (HUD) oversees the Federal Housing Administration (FHA); the U. S. Department for Veterans Affairs oversees VA loans. All are regulated in some way by the federal government; their provisions can be changed or amended by Congress. The foregoing information was current when this book went to print.

OWNER-FINANCING ARRANGEMENTS

Unlike the foregoing loans, owner-financing arrangements do not have guidelines for down payments or credit scores or debt-to-income ratios, nor do they have underwriting requirements. If a buyer and a seller want to engage in a private owner-financed arrangement, there are certain, common-sense guidelines to follow, but generally no required financial guidelines. It is up to the parties involved in the owner-financing arrangement to agree upon the terms of the contract.

Owner-Financing Arrangements may be used for owner-occupied property or for residential and/or commercial investment property or for raw land. The borrower and the seller come to an agreement regarding the price of the property, the period of the loan, the down payment, and the terms regarding the agreement.

There are no mortgage insurance premiums that are paid by the borrower; and there is no loan guarantee for the seller who is financing the property. There are, however, options available to the seller/owner, in case the buyer/borrower defaults on the loan.

CHAPTER 2

THREE DIFFERENT TYPES OF OWNER-FINANCING ARRANGEMENTS

Since the banks, mortgage lenders, and mortgage companies have tightened up their loan requirements, private money has become an alternative source of funds for individuals who buy and sell real estate.

In New Mexico, three common owner-financing arrangements are used: Mortgages, Deeds of Trust, and Real Estate Contracts. These different types of arrangements are briefly described in this chapter.

PROMISSORY NOTE AND MORTGAGE

In a mortgage, there are two parties to the arrangement, the seller who owns the property and the buyer. The buyer executes a promissory note in favor of the seller which outlines the amount borrowed, the term of the note, the interest rate on the note, the frequency of payment on the note, what constitutes default on the note, and the seller's remedy for default. The seller turns over the deed to the property to the buyer at this time.

Concurrent with the promissory note, the seller executes a mortgage on the property outlined in the promissory note; and this mortgage is filed with the county in which the property is located. This mortgage identifies the real estate

Chapter 2

as collateral or security for the promissory note. The seller holds the mortgage while the buyer makes payments. At the end of the term of the note, the seller releases the mortgage and the buyer owns the property free and clear. It is then the buyer's responsibility to have a release of the mortgage recorded.

The mortgage generally contains a clause called an acceleration clause that allows the seller to demand the entire balance of the loan if the buyer defaults on the loan. If the buyer doesn't pay, the seller may begin foreclosure proceedings which take place in the court system.

The seller does not necessarily have to notify the buyer that foreclosure is being initiated, but after the foreclosure complaint is filed with the Court, the seller is required to notify the buyer. This foreclosure process generally could take up to six months or more. Once the property is foreclosed, the auction of that property takes place on the courthouse steps and the property is sold to the highest bidder.

With a mortgage, the buyer has a right of redemption that allows the buyer to redeem the foreclosed property by paying back the seller the unpaid balance on the loan. If foreclosure has already occurred and the property has been sold at auction, the buyer would have the right to redeem the property by paying back the auction buyer whatever was paid for the property at auction, plus interest of 10%.[(2015 New Mexico Statutes, Chapter 39, Article 5, Section 39-5-18, A. (1)]. This redemption right is valid for a certain period of time; and in New Mexico, this redemption right may run from 30 to 270 days. [(2015 New Mexico Statutes, Chapter

39, Article 5, Section 39-5-18, A. (1) and New Mexico Statutes, Chapter 39, Article 5, Section 39-5-19)]

When using a promissory note and mortgage, the seller generally would want to enlist the services of an escrow agent or third-party processor to keep track of the interest accrued and payments as they are made.

A WORD ABOUT REDEMPTION RIGHTS…

I have two stories to share regarding redemption rights. It is not uncommon for individuals to sell their redemption rights on their mortgage.

In one instance, I was at an auction on the courthouse steps and was prepared to bid on a property. Shortly before the bidding process began for this property, an individual circulated among the assembled crowd telling everyone that he owned the redemption rights to that property. Due to the way these rights operate, I decided it would not be a prudent decision to bid on the property in question, because I would be unable to do anything with that property until the redemption rights expire.

Piggybacking on the previous story, in another instance, I owned the redemption rights on a foreclosed property. The foreclosed property was bought by an individual who chose not to wait for the redemption rights to expire, before setting about making improvements on the property, such as new carpeting and painting. I exercised the redemption rights and bought the property for the auction price plus interest, as was my right. Since the auction buyer had made improvements on the property at no cost to me, we eventually came to a monetary agreement that made us both happy.

PROMISSORY NOTE AND TRUST DEEDS

With this arrangement, the buyer of the property executes a promissory note to the owner or seller of the property. As in the mortgage arrangement previously described, the promissory note outlines the amount borrowed, the term of the note, the interest rate on the note, the frequency of payment on the note, what constitutes default on the note, and the seller's remedy for default. The deed for the property is transferred to the buyer and a trust deed is executed at that time.

With a trust deed, there are three parties involved: the buyer (called the trustor), the seller (called the beneficiary), and the trustee which is a third party, such as an attorney, title company, or escrow agent. The trust deed is then filed with the county to identify that the property is collateral or security for the promissory note. The trust deed operates in the same fashion as the mortgage, previously described.

When the buyer has fulfilled the obligation of repaying the note in full, the trust deed is released and the buyer owns the property free and clear. It is the buyer's responsibility to have the release of the trust deed recorded.

As with a mortgage, the trust deed contains an acceleration clause for the seller to notify the trustee to implement foreclosure proceedings if the buyer/borrower defaults on the loan. There is also a redemption clause for the buyer/borrower to pay back the seller the unpaid balance on the loan, allowing the buyer to redeem the foreclosed property.

Although trust deeds are designed to avoid the judicial process of foreclosure inherent in a mortgage, New Mexico statutes require the trustee to implement foreclosure proceedings similar in manner as with a mortgage. The foreclosure process with a trust deed generally takes less time to accomplish than with a mortgage, however.

Be aware that some banks require judicial foreclosure on a property before they will lend again on that property. In addition, title companies may not insure the property without evidence of a judicial foreclosure.

With a promissory note and trust deed, the seller generally would want an escrow agent or third-party processor to keep track of the payments.

REAL ESTATE CONTRACT

A real estate contract is a legally enforceable agreement between the seller of real property and the buyer of the real property, executed when the sale of the property occurs. Both the seller and buyer agree to the terms of the contract. The contract outlines the amount borrowed, the term of the note, the interest rate on the note, the frequency of payment on the note, what constitutes default on the note, and the seller's remedy for default.

At the time of contract execution, the seller/owner completes a warranty deed conveying title to the real property to the buyer. The buyer/borrower executes a special warranty deed conveying the title of the real property back to the seller/owner. Neither of these deeds are filed with the county, but both deeds are held by the escrow agent until such time as the agreement is paid in full or the buyer/borrower defaults.

In addition, a memorandum of real estate contract may be filed with the county to notify parties that there is a contract outstanding and to prevent either party from going around the other in the sale of the real property. In effect, this memorandum of real estate contract "clouds" the title of the real property.

If the buyer/borrower defaults on the payments, the seller/owner generally has recourse to one of two remedies. The seller/owner may have a *demand* letter sent asking the buyer to *cure* the default, generally within 30 days; or the seller/owner may activate the acceleration clause and sue for the balance of the loan due on the contract.

Under the demand letter approach, if the buyer/borrower does not cure the default, the seller/owner presents the escrow agent with an affidavit of default and obtains the special warranty deed executed by the buyer/borrower at the time the contract was signed. The seller/owner can then file this special warranty deed and the affidavit of default with the county, thereby again assuming title to the real property.

Under the acceleration-of-the-balance-due approach, the buyer/borrower is required to pay off the loan in full or faces judicial foreclosure. After payment, the buyer/borrower receives both the warranty deed and the special warranty deed from the escrow agent. It is the buyer/borrower's responsibility to file the warranty deed with the county and assume title to the real property. In my experience, I have only heard of this acceleration-of-the-balance-due-approach being used once.

If the buyer/borrower defaults, there are no foreclosure proceedings that take place. Generally speaking, the only time the buyer may go to court would be to sue for the equity that one has built up in the property referenced in the real estate contract.

For the balance of this book, I will focus on real estate contracts in depth, including their appeal, their viability in certain situations, potential areas where pitfalls may arise, and the key provisions that may be contained in each contract.

CHAPTER 3

EFFICIENCY OF REAL ESTATE CONTRACTS

In my opinion, Real Estate Contracts are the most efficient of the owner-financing arrangements; and this book will focus on Real Estate Contracts from an Escrow Agent's point of view. Real Estate Contracts can make buying or selling a property a lot less complicated.

As stated in the last chapter, using private money for the purchase or sale of real estate has become increasingly popular, since banks and other mortgage lending institutions tightened their loan requirements. More stringent loan requirements not only pertain to credit scores and the amount of down payment required, but also may encompass the documentation required to qualify for the loan. In addition, the total number of mortgages an individual may have may be limited.

These loan requirements impact buyers and sellers, alike, since the requirements limit the number of potential buyers from the seller's pool of possible candidates. Borrowers who otherwise may not qualify for a loan at a lending institution may enter into a Real Estate Contract to purchase the property. Owners are able to sell their property using an expedited process. This makes Real Estate Contracts a good option for both the seller and the buyer.

REASONS WHY A BUYER MAY NOT QUALIFY

To some, the inability to qualify for a loan may raise a red flag. There are many reasons why a borrower may not qualify for conventional financing. It is noted that being unable to qualify does not necessarily equate to a bad credit risk or a "deadbeat."

Let's take a moment to review some of the criteria that lending institutions require when qualifying a borrower for a loan.

Income/Employment

A borrower's income must be substantial enough to cover all of the borrower's obligations.

As part of this review, the lending institution looks at the borrower's debt-to-income ratio. For a conventional, conforming loan, a borrower's debt-to-income ratio generally should be about 36%; for an FHA loan, the debt-to-income ratio generally may be as high as 43%. This ratio looks at the borrower's total monthly consumer-debt obligations divided by the borrower's total monthly gross income to arrive at the percentage.

In establishing income, a borrower generally is asked to provide three months' worth of pay stubs. This requirement can exclude borrowers who are new to their position or may have a lucrative position lined up, but have not yet started.

Verifying income for a self-employed individual can be a challenge as well, since the self-employed individual is not able to bring in three months' worth of pay stubs. Instead, the self-employed person is generally required to bring in one's income tax returns for the last two or three years.

Chapter 3

A challenge arises since self-employed individuals have numerous write-offs or deductions that may be used in connection with a business. These income tax returns generally may not reflect the borrower's true household income. Further, the self-employed individual who is just starting a business may be unable to show any income for several years.

What about the borrower who has substantial assets, is living off of those assets, yet has no income? A mortgage lender shared the story of a successful individual who relocated to New Mexico, after selling his own television/film-editing business.

This individual decided he did not want to start another business right away and was living off substantial proceeds from the sale of his previous business. He was not old enough to draw his pension or social security income, so he was showing no income. Although his assets were substantial, under the current qualification criteria, this individual could not qualify for a loan.

Credit Score

FICO is the name given to the score that is used to rank an individual's credit risk. It is named after the Fair Isaac Corporation which was the first company to develop a credit-risk model. It is used by the three credit bureaus which compile and maintain an individual's credit history.

FICO scores do not take an individual's income or assets into consideration. An individual could have substantial debt that is all secured by assets of greater value than the debt, in other words, equity. The score only looks at the amount of debt.

Further, an individual may have more than enough income to service one's debt, but the FICO calculation does not take that into account. So, in effect, a low FICO score may not necessarily say anything adverse about a borrower.

The borrower's FICO score plays an important part in the qualification process, however; and the borrower is assumed to be a better credit risk if the score is high. This may present a problem to some individuals who may not have any credit or may have bad credit.

Younger borrowers may not have established credit, yet, managing to use a debit card for all their purchases. In addition, younger individuals may still be carried on another individual's credit card, such as a parent's credit card, as an associate card holder. Any credit history would accrue to the owner's or parent's record, and not the associate's record.

Surprising as it may seem, there are individuals who have never established credit, but have paid cash for all of their acquisitions. Regardless of whether the borrower is young and has not established credit or more mature and has conscientiously decided not to establish credit, these individuals would not have a credit score. It would be difficult to qualify for a loan.

There are also individuals who may have poor credit. Poor credit affects the credit score. There may be a history of paying late or not paying at all; the credit cards may be over extended, with credit-card limits being maxed out and only the interest being paid.

There may be situations in which one spouse has good credit, and the other spouse has poor credit. (I doubt that credit reports come up in the courting process.) The approval could fail due to the fact that the incomes of both spouses are needed in order to qualify, but only the spouse with good credit could apply for the loan.

An individual may co-sign on a loan for another individual without knowing the ramifications of this act. Co-signers guarantee the debt of the borrower, and if that borrower fails to pay, it is the Co-signer's responsibility to pay the debt. Co-signers may be ill prepared to take over a loan and be unable to make payments for which one had not planned. Individuals unknowingly get themselves into situations such as this all the time, and this has a negative impact on their credit score.

There may be a foreclosure or bankruptcy on an individual's credit report due to a failed business venture, lengthy illness, or catastrophic medical bills. Even though individuals may take steps to clean up their credit report since an event occurred, there are a certain number of years that must elapse before these events are removed from a credit report. Lenders also require that a number of years elapse since the event, before they will consider qualifying the borrower for a loan.

Assets On Deposit

Typically, lenders also require borrowers to have at least two to three months' worth of living expenses in the form of savings on deposit in order to qualify for a loan. This money has to be the borrower's own money that one has accrued and cannot be the result of a gift.

Lenders recognize that buying real estate is no doubt the biggest expenditure an individual may make. They want to ensure that there are reserves set aside so that the borrower will be able to make the loan payments, as well as maintain the property and make any needed repairs.

Too Many Mortgages

Banks and lending institutions may limit the number of mortgages that an individual may carry, even though the individual is able to qualify for the loan.

I have personal experience with this. I placed earnest money on a piece of property that was out of state, and upon my return to Albuquerque proceeded to secure a mortgage from my bank. Imagine my surprise when the bank told me I was unable to qualify because I had the maximum number of mortgages they allowed which I believe was four. Undaunted, I began shopping other banks and found one that would approve my mortgage. This particular bank would allow individuals to carry 10 mortgages, and I was able to go through with the purchase.

In summary, Real Estate Contracts can allow a whole group of borrowers who may be excluded by the lending industry but who have the ability to pay, the opportunity to participate in real estate property ownership.

CHAPTER 4

ADVANTAGES OF USING REAL ESTATE CONTRACTS

It is easy to get into a Real Estate Contract, and just as easy to extricate oneself from a Real Estate Contract. The buyer/borrower does not have to qualify for the loan, does not have a federally-regulated down payment, and does not have to pay Private Mortgage Insurance or a Mortgage Insurance Premium.

The buyer/borrower and the seller/owner just need to come to an agreement on the amount of the down payment and the repayment terms. This contract is legally enforceable which means that the agreement may be enforced by the Courts if the parties do not honor the terms of the agreement.

After the Real Estate Contract is signed, the buyer/borrower should understand that as long as the payments are made and the loan is paid in full, one will end up with the deed to the property. The buyer/borrower should also understand that if one defaults on the loan, the property could either be taken back by the seller/owner and the buyer/borrower will forfeit any money paid into the Real Estate Contract; or the seller/owner may accelerate payment of the balance due on the loan.

The seller/owner enters into the contract expecting that payments will be made until the loan is paid in full; as an added attraction, the seller/owner may enjoy a stream of income from these payments.

If the buyer/borrower defaults on the loan, the seller/owner may take back the property, keep the down payment and any other loan payments, and reclaim title to the property. The seller/owner knows that one can accomplish this through sending the buyer/borrower a letter and does not typically have to go through lengthy and costly foreclosure proceedings in the Court.

Alternatively, if the seller/owner decides to accelerate the balance due on the loan, the seller/owner would sue for the balance of the loan.

It is noted that Real Estate Contracts are not for everyone; they may work in some situations and not work in others. For example, a seller/owner may need the proceeds from the sale of the property to use as a down payment on the purchase of another property; and a Real Estate Contract may not be viable. In this chapter, I review the advantages to both the buyer and the seller.

ADVANTAGES TO THE SELLER

As stated in the previous chapter, a seller who is willing to consider a Real Estate Contract expands the pool of potential buyers.

If the seller does not need the cash from the sales proceeds immediately, a Real Estate Contract can provide a stream of monthly income. This stream of income generally may be anywhere from four percent to five percent higher than the income generated by a certificate of deposit. Although there is risk with any investment, I am of the opinion that a Real Estate Contract, if created carefully, generally may be viewed as a secure investment.

From a seller's point of view, the sale of the property is expedited and can take place immediately. There is no appraisal or inspection report required for the sale to take place. Of course, an inspection or appraisal could take place if these items are written into the terms of the purchase agreement.

A seller may receive a higher purchase price on the property with a Real Estate Contract. Since the buyer may have a smaller down payment than one would have with a conventional mortgage and does not have to pay origination points or discount points on the loan, the buyer may be willing to pay a higher purchase price.

In order to ensure compliance with the agreement and ascertain that the buyer is serious about the purchase, the seller may request a reasonable down payment amount. As an Escrow Agent, I have seen down payments of 10%, for example. The amount of down payment is not indicative of the success of the contract, however.

I have also seen a Real Estate Contract with a 20% down payment default, while a Contract with no money down paid off early. Remember, the buyer loses the down payment and any payments made to date if the buyer defaults on the Real Estate Contract.

Since the buyer does not have to qualify for the loan, one may be willing to pay a slightly higher interest rate on the Real Estate Contract. It's been my experience to see generally 100 to 400 basis points more than the going mortgage interest rate.

In case of default, the seller does not typically have to go through lengthy, judicial foreclosure proceedings to take back the property. If the buyer is in default, the seller's attorney sends a demand letter giving the buyer generally 30 days to cure the default. The Real Estate Contract outlines that the buyer pays the attorney's cost for drafting the letter. After the cure default period, if the buyer has not cured the default, the seller may take back the property.

Note that the seller is not required to have an attorney write the letter, but the letter must contain specific language defining what is demanded and the time frame to cure. Further, if an attorney is not used for the demand letter, the attorney's fee referenced in the Contract to be charged to, and paid for by the buyer, cannot be charged. As a general rule, I strongly recommend using an attorney in all real estate-related matters.

ADVANTAGES TO THE BUYER

A Real Estate Contract allows buyers who otherwise may not qualify for a conventional loan the opportunity to purchase real property. This includes buyers who may be new in a job; have no credit or bad credit; have substantial assets, but no income; or whose assets are highly leveraged.

The Real Estate Contract allows buyers the time to establish or improve their credit scores, employment history, or assets, so that they may qualify for a conventional mortgage. Buyers should try to move in this direction in case there is a future balloon payment due on the Real Estate Contract in three to five years, or as a means to reduce their interest rate.

Buyers, especially those who are self-employed, may not want to go through the hassle of the loan application process in order to qualify. They are able to avoid that process by using a Real Estate Contract.

Real Estate Contracts usually do not appear on an individual's credit report. This may appeal to investors in property, since the banks limit the number of mortgages an individual may have, even though the individual is able to qualify for the loan.

Buyers with lower down payments can avoid paying Private Mortgage Insurance or Mortgage Insurance Premiums.

There are no origination fees or discount points attached to the loan, nor are there closing fees and mortgage company documentation preparation fees.

The buyer is able to take possession of the property and is able to make improvements on the property.

With a Real Estate Contract, the buyer can pay off the contract at any time without penalty, since it appears a seller in the state of New Mexico generally is unable to enforce a prepayment penalty on residential real estate. [(2015 New Mexico Statutes, Chapter 56, Article 8, Section 56-8-30)].

While payments are required to be made on time and a payment is deemed to be late one day after the payment is due, it is possible for the buyer to call the seller to explain the circumstances. If the seller knows that the buyer is not trying to default on the contract, the seller may not move to execute the terms of the contract by sending a demand letter.

ADVANTAGES TO BOTH

A Real Estate Contract is a viable way to sell to tenants who are currently residing on the property. The buyer/tenant already has established a track record for payment, and the seller may generally feel more confident that the tenants will maintain that track record when they enter into a Real Estate Contract.

The terms of the Real Estate Contract are created to suit the needs of both parties; i.e., the due date for the payments does not have to be on the first of the month, but may be on another date that is convenient to both parties. Further, the payments could be scheduled other than monthly, for example, quarterly or semi-annually.

Real Estate Contracts are flexible; the payment date and terms of the Real Estate Contract may change at some future date, providing both parties agree to this and execute the appropriate written modifications.

Terry Tip:
In my opinion, the real value of a Real Estate Contract is that a buyer/borrower can talk directly with the seller/owner in case a situation arises. This is different from a mortgage company where it is next to impossible to talk with anyone who can make a decision.

If a buyer/borrower is going to be late with a payment due to sickness or being laid off from a job, that individual is able to speak with the seller/owner directly to explain the situation. Alternatively, if the seller/owner is relying on the buyer/borrower's payment to make the payment on an underlying obligation, the seller/owner can communicate that, as well. A Real Estate Contract can allow the parties to have dialogue with one another in meeting challenges and come to an agreeable solution.

It's been my experience that a seller/owner just wants to know the payment is coming, rather than jumping to the conclusion when the payment is late that the buyer/borrower has fled the country and the property is in a state of disrepair! That is the value of the Real Estate Contract—the ability to talk to a person who has a vested interest in the property and can make a decision, rather than a servicer at the end of a toll-free number who cannot make a decision.

POSSIBLE DISADVANTAGES

FOR THE SELLER

Under a Real Estate Contract, the seller may receive less of a down payment from the buyer than could be expected from a buyer who takes the route of a conventional mortgage.

The income stream from the Real Estate Contract generated by the buyer's payments typically has more risk than a pension or Social Security or bank investment.

Further, if a seller/owner engages in the selling of multiple residential properties which are owner-financed during a 12-month period, the seller/owner may be subject to the Dodd-Frank Wall Street Reform and Consumer Protection Act. There are some exceptions to the provisions of this Act that apply, and a seller/owner is strongly urged to consult with one's attorney.

FOR THE BUYER

A buyer under a Real Estate Contract may unknowingly assume the seller's lien on the property. This could happen if the seller was unaware of the existence of a lien and if the buyer did not perform a title search. This is a good reason to always obtain title insurance at closing.

The buyer may not receive monthly statements regarding the status of the loan, and interest paid, if the seller performs the administration of the contract, rather than having an escrow agent perform the administration.

FOR BOTH

Although the Real Estate Contract is a legally enforceable contract, the legal process is less defined than it is with a judicial foreclosure. In effect, the parties rely on the documents written by an attorney, rather than federal regulations attached to conventional financing. It is important that the Real Estate Contract be prepared by a real estate attorney so that both parties are protected and there is less chance for ambiguities.

In the next chapter, we cover the parties involved in a Real Estate Contract.

CHAPTER 5

PARTIES TO A REAL ESTATE CONTRACT

In the last several chapters, I've used the terms buyer and seller, and those are the two parties to the Real Estate Contract.

It is my opinion that an individual seeking to buy or sell real estate under a Real Estate Contract (Contract) should have a team of licensed professionals upon whom to call.

Since this book is written to be useful to professionals and non-professionals alike, I will identify the parties on this team, and the role that each one may play.

SELLER

As previously discussed, the seller is an individual or entity who holds legal title to the property and enters into the Real Estate Contract with the buyer. A seller may own the property free and clear or there may be a mortgage outstanding. Later in this book, I will cover the way in which Real Estate Contracts are used in each situation.

It is noted that the seller on the Contract may not sell only the property, but may also sell the right to receive the income on the Real Estate Contract, thereby turning the Contract into a marketable investment.

For example, let's say a seller enters into a Real Estate Contract with a buyer. Generally, after the down payment, the seller may fully expect to enjoy the income stream that is generated. Several years into the Contract, however, the seller may require substantial cash, perhaps for medical bills or a business opportunity.

Generally speaking, there is no provision in the Contract that would permit the seller to rescind the Contract without cause, take back the property, and then sell it to another buyer for the needed cash. Termination or rescission, with taking back the property, is a remedy only upon default; and this is not a default situation. In this instance, the seller may sell the income rights attached to the Real Estate Contract.

In effect, the owner executes a seller's assignment of income and legal title to the property to a third party. Since the owner has already received several years' worth of payments, chances are the Contract is not sold at face value, but at a discount.

After the income rights are sold, the individual who purchases these rights receives the monthly payments as they are made on the Contract; the seller named in the Contract receives an immediate, discounted pay-off for the price of the property; and the buyer named in the Contract who continues to make payments, will receive the title to the property at the time the Contract is paid off.

BUYER

The buyer is an individual who enters into the Real Estate Contract with the seller. After making payments according to the terms of the Contract, the buyer receives legal title to the property. The buyer may be an individual who desires to live in the property that is purchased or may be an individual or entity that buys the property for investment.

As with the seller and depending on the specific wording of the Real Estate Contract, the buyer of the property may subsequently sell one's interest in the property to another purchaser. The new purchaser would then make the payments under the existing Real Estate Contract, and would get title to the property upon paying off the Contract.

A buyer may enter into a Real Estate Contract in instances wherein one does not know whether one will complete its terms.

If the buyer defaults and the seller takes back the property, the buyer's credit is usually not adversely affected. Alternatively, if the buyer defaults and the seller sues for the balance due on the loan under the acceleration provision, this could have an adverse effect on the buyer's credit. Although suing for the loan balance is an option, experience has shown that sellers generally take back the property.

For example, when I was in college, I purchased a large piece of property through a Real Estate Contract. My plan was to subdivide this property into mobile-home lots. In order to do that, however, I would need to get the zoning laws changed; and I was uncertain whether or not I could get this accomplished.

As it turns out, I was unable to get the zoning laws changed and I let the property go back to the seller. The only thing I lost was my down payment and several subsequent payments. This default had no impact on my credit at all.

Now that I have more experience in the buying and selling of real estate, I recognize that I could have bought an option to buy the real estate in the foregoing example and would have avoided a default situation. I did not comprehend that at the time; and luckily, the seller took back the property.

Recalling the ease with which a buyer may enter into a Real Estate Contract and the remedy for the seller in case the buyer defaults, it is noted that Real Estate Contracts may be used frequently in Self-Directed Individual Retirement Accounts (IRAs).

When real estate is purchased for a Self-Directed IRA, the type of loan that may be used is a *non-recourse* loan. A non-recourse loan is one in which the asset is the only item that secures the loan; the lender cannot go after the IRA's assets, nor can the lender go after the assets of the IRA owner.

Hence, if the Custodian for a Self-Directed IRA enters into a Real Estate Contract as the buyer, and the Contract has been written without an acceleration provision; this makes the Real Estate Contract a non-recourse loan.

Upon default, the only remedy the seller has is to take back the property. This is consistent with the Internal Revenue Code that governs Individual Retirement Accounts, and can make the use of Real Estate Contracts attractive in Self-Directed IRA scenarios.

REAL ESTATE PROFESSIONAL

Whether buying or selling an owner-occupied residence or an investment property, it is my opinion that the services of a real estate professional are invaluable and necessary.

Real Estate Professionals are familiar with local laws, schools, neighborhoods, and trends in the industry; they have experience and may possibly recognize issues before those issues are discovered in an inspection.

A primary function is to act in the role of an intermediary between the seller of property and the buyer of the property. Real Estate Professionals may also serve as liaison with the title company, the appraiser (when applicable), and with the inspection representatives.

A Real Estate Professional who represents the seller of the property is referred to as a listing agent. In the case of a Real Estate Contract, the Real Estate Professional would ask the seller questions regarding what the seller plans to do with the sales proceeds to determine if a Real Estate Contract is viable.

The Real Estate Professional who represents the buyer of the property is referred to as a buyer's agent, and in the case of a Real Estate Contract, would look at the Multiple Listing Service (MLS) indicating that the seller can finance the property.

In the case of Real Estate Contracts, it is wise for Real Estate Professionals to have a broad knowledge of the way in which contracts operate, and the importance of certain provisions therein, so that they may counsel their respective clients. As a point of information, Real Estate Professionals should not offer legal advice, but it is important to be able to discuss these provisions, and then refer the client to a Real Estate Attorney.

The Realtors® Association of New Mexico provides a form titled Addendum to Purchase Agreement-Real Estate Contract that may be used to describe the important provisions and terms that should be inserted into a Real

Estate Contract by an attorney. This form may be used by Realtors® who are able to access it and share its contents with their clients.

REAL ESTATE ATTORNEY

It is noted that each state has its own requirements regarding a Real Estate Attorney's involvement with the sale and purchase of a property. Some states will not allow a transaction unless a Real Estate Attorney is involved. Although New Mexico does not have such a law, in the case of a Real Estate Contract, I highly recommend engaging the services of a Real Estate Attorney before signing any Contract.

A Real Estate Attorney is familiar with the laws that govern Real Estate Contracts, as well as the key provisions that need to be included in the Contract to protect the seller and the buyer. The Real Estate Attorney will write the Real Estate Contract according to the terms to which both parties have agreed. These terms are outlined on the Purchase Agreement and may be outlined on an Addendum to Purchase Agreement-Real Estate Contract or a comparable document. A properly-drawn Real Estate Contract will allow both parties to feel comfortable in moving forward.

Generally speaking, Real Estate Professionals, Title Company Representatives, and Escrow Agents have a broad working knowledge regarding New Mexico real estate laws, and are no doubt able to handle some basic questions pertaining to a Real Estate Contract; however, they are not allowed to give legal advice. A situation may occur wherein a Real Estate Professional or an Escrow Agent tells a client something that is legally factual, but the client's situation doesn't fit the statement of fact. Chances are the Real Estate

Chapter 5

Professional or Escrow Agent may not know the client's entire situation. This is where the services of an attorney are required.

From a Real Estate Professional's or Escrow Agent's point of view, it is always best to have an attorney to whom the client can be referred. Further, it is my opinion that one should always advise the client to go to a Real Estate Attorney for the review of any documents and to answer any questions.

CERTIFIED PUBLIC ACCOUNTANT (CPA)

CPAs can be invaluable when an individual sells a property. They are able to advise an individual of the appropriate taxation on the sale of the property, and how to structure the sale of the property. They may also advise on the subsequent purchase of another piece of property so that it may qualify for a tax-free exchange under Internal Revenue Code Section 1031, if applicable.

In my opinion, a CPA is necessary for individuals who are in the real estate business; by this I mean individuals who buy and sell properties for profit. CPAs stay abreast of all the tax laws to allow individuals to maximize their deductions on properties. In addition, CPAs can prepare a cash flow analysis to determine if an individual can afford the additional cost of another property; this is especially helpful for individuals who are highly leveraged.

TITLE COMPANY

A Title Company is a key player for the team of professionals. It is my opinion that property should not be bought or sold without a Title Company. This is my first rule.

The Title Company performs a search to ascertain that the individual or the entity who is claiming to be the owner of the property and is selling the property actually has legal title to the property. In addition to property ownership, this research covers outstanding liens or judgments, unpaid taxes, restrictions or easements, and unpaid Association dues, as well as unpaid water bills which attach to the property in New Mexico.

Further, the Title Company can issue a Title Insurance Policy that protects the lender (which in the case of the Real Estate Contract is the seller of the property) and the "new owner" (which in the case of the Real Estate Contract is the buyer of the property) against claims or legal fees arising from a dispute with the title or fraudulent ownership claims.

Based upon the opening paragraph of this section, it would seem that I never buy or sell property without a Title Company. Allow me to share the story of the one time I did not close through a Title Company.

I entered into a Real Estate Contract with my sister-in-law to buy the house in which she was living. She furnished the legal description of the property, the Contract was drawn up, signed, and recorded. Since it was my sister-in-law, I didn't bother closing with a Title Company.

After I began making payments, I received a phone call from a former associate who worked at the County Clerk's Office; and referencing the recorded Contract with my sister-in-law, he advised me that a "lady was trying to sell me property she didn't own."

We discovered that my sister-in-law inadvertently had used the legal address of a property she previously owned and sold, and not the legal description of the property that was the subject of the Real Estate Contract we both signed.

Had I continued down this route and ultimately paid off the Contract, I would have purchased a property to which I did not have legal title. In addition, this action would have clouded the buyer's title of the property previously sold by my sister-in-law.

That is an illustration that points out why closing with a Title Company is so important.

ESCROW AGENT

In New Mexico, Real Estate Contracts have evolved so that Escrow Agents are used as independent third parties in just about all Real Estate Contract situations. As a point of information however, individuals are not required to use an Escrow Agent.

The Escrow Agent receives the monthly payments of the buyer and distributes them according to the terms of the Contract; calculates principal and interest, as well as the principal balance; and can hold money for taxes and insurance in an impound account to pay the taxes and insurance when due. The Escrow Agent issues the Internal Revenue Service's Form 1098 Mortgage Interest Statement to the buyer that shows the amount of interest paid by the borrower on the Real Estate Contract.

Escrow Agents are regulated and licensed by the Financial Institutions Division of the New Mexico Regulation and Licensing Department. In this respect, Escrow Agents must pay for a license, reapply for a license every year, maintain a $100,000.00 bond, and follow the regulations applicable to Escrow companies.

An Escrow Agent must deposit any money coming into an escrow account into a separate trust account managed by a bank, a savings and loan institution, or a credit union located in New Mexico, prior to disbursing any money. The State of New Mexico audits Escrow Agents about every 12 to 18 months or so to ensure that these trust accounts balance, and that the Escrow Agent's operations are in order.

As an interested party to a Real Estate Contract, if there are any concerns with the way in which the Escrow Agent is handling the account, I strongly encourage individuals to call the Escrow Agent directly to try to clear up the issue. If that does not work, individuals may file a complaint with the Financial Institutions Division.

When this route is taken, the Financial Institutions Division forwards the complaint to the Escrow Agent requesting the Escrow Agent's side of the story. The Financial Institutions Division acts as intermediary between the two parties until the complaint is resolved.

Note that the Escrow Agent does not need to be in the same county as the property, nor even in the same state as the property.

Now that the parties to a Real Estate Contract are identified, let's identify the components of a Real Estate Contract.

CHAPTER 6

COMPONENTS OF A REAL ESTATE CONTRACT

THE SALE

In order to have a Real Estate Contract (Contract), there must be a sale of real property. It is not possible to have a Real Estate Contract on a boat, for example; nor is it possible to have a Real Estate Contract on a mobile home, unless that mobile home is permanently attached to a piece of real estate. Note that a mobile home is considered personal property, rather than real property.

For the sale, the buyer/borrower agrees to buy the piece of property on an installment basis from the seller/owner. These installments may be monthly, quarterly, semi-annually, or even annually. The term of the contract may be any number of years—as short as one year and typically not more than 30 years. The interest rate used to calculate the payments is stated in the Contract, as well.

Upon entering into the Real Estate Contract, the seller/owner retains legal title to the property; this allows the seller/owner the ability to take legal action against anyone attempting to infringe upon one's ownership rights.

The buyer/borrower receives what is known as *equitable title*. Equitable title is an individual's right to use and enjoy the property. An individual with equitable title may obtain full legal title to the property by abiding by the terms of the Contract. In effect, equitable title confers a financial interest in the property, and the buyer/borrower does not obtain the legal title to the property until the Contract is paid in full.

As stated previously, a buyer/borrower with equitable title may make improvements to the property as if one already owns it. Any appreciation in the property over the course of the Contract accrues to the benefit of the buyer/borrower.

THE REAL ESTATE CONTRACT

There are certain provisions that are included in most Real Estate Contracts, and I will review them briefly in this chapter. Later in this book, I will discuss these provisions in detail.

Name of the Seller and Buyer

This is the name in which the seller/owner holds title to the property and the name in which the buyer/borrower wishes to hold title to the property.

Address

The Real Estate Contract shows the address of the property that is being purchased, as well as the legal description of the property.

Way In Which the Property Is Owned

This provision indicates the way in which the buyer/borrower wants the property to be titled, and who may inherit the property at the buyer/borrower's death.

Price and Payments

This provision outlines the amount of the Contract and includes any obligations the buyer/borrower may assume;

the amount of the down payment; and the balance that is due the seller/owner.

The details of the Contract are included in this provision and include the frequency of payment, the interest rate and the frequency with which the interest is charged, the term of the Contract, the starting date of the Contract, and the ending date of the Contract.

The time in which a payment is deemed to be late is outlined in this provision, as well as the late-charge fee to be paid by the buyer.

Prior Obligations

Any prior liens or obligations that are attached to the property are outlined, and the individual responsible for paying these prior obligations, either the buyer/borrower or the seller/owner, will be listed. This provision also indicates whether the buyer/borrower and/or seller/owner will pay the obligations directly or will employ the services of an Escrow Agent to pay those obligations.

Property Maintenance, Insurance, and Taxes

This provision requires the buyer/borrower to maintain the property in good condition, carry insurance on the property, and pay the taxes on the property. It includes information regarding whether the buyer/borrower will create a new escrow account, use an existing escrow account, if applicable; or pay the property taxes and hazard insurance directly. Note, if the buyer/borrower does not conform to this provision of the Contract, this may trigger a default on the Contract.

Right to Transfer or Sell the Property

This provision stipulates whether the buyer/borrower must obtain prior approval from the seller/owner to transfer the property to someone else. If the transfer requires prior approval from the seller/owner and the buyer/borrower does not obtain the approval, this action may trigger a default on the Contract.

Default

This provision outlines the period of time in which the buyer/borrower has to cure the default. It is noted that a buyer/borrower who does not conform to the terms of the Contract may enter into a default situation.

Upon a default situation, a "demand" letter (generally prepared by an attorney) is sent to the buyer/borrower in which the default is outlined and the buyer/borrower is given a number of days to correct the default situation. Contracts typically show a 30-day cure default provision, but the number of days may be longer than this. If the buyer/borrower does not comply, the seller/owner may take steps to take the property back or sue for the full amount due.

In this provision, it also is indicated the buyer/borrower will pay the cost of having the attorney prepare a demand letter, and the cost for this is stated.

Escrow Agent and Fees

This provision names the Escrow Agent for the Real Estate Contract (if applicable) and outlines the Escrow Agent's fees to be paid by the buyer/borrower and those to be paid by the seller/owner.

Chapter 6

Optional Provisions

The Real Estate Contract may contain some optional provisions, such as a provision for obtaining an appraisal or an inspection, as well as the seller/owner requesting complete financial disclosure from the buyer/borrower, or at a minimum, a credit report.

Contract Signatures

The terms of the Real Estate Contract are agreed to by both parties, and both the seller/owner and the buyer/borrower sign the Contract. The Contract is also notarized. Upon execution of the Contract, it is filed with the County Clerk's Office and may become public information. Alternatively, a Memorandum of Real Estate Contract may be filed with the County Clerk's Office, in lieu of the full Real Estate Contract.

WARRANTY DEED

Upon executing a Real Estate Contract, the seller/owner of the property executes a warranty deed giving legal title of the property to the buyer/borrower. The warranty deed is notarized.

The warranty deed sets forth that the seller/owner has the legal title to the property.

This deed is not recorded, but is held in escrow while the buyer/borrower makes payments. Upon successful completion of the Real Estate Contract, the seller/owner instructs the Escrow Agent to turn over the warranty deed to the buyer/borrower, and it is then the buyer/borrower's responsibility to have the warranty deed recorded.

SPECIAL WARRANTY DEED

Concurrent with executing the Real Estate Contract, the buyer/borrower of the property executes a special warranty deed giving legal title of the property back to the seller/owner. The special warranty deed is notarized. This deed is not recorded, but is held by the Escrow Agent while the buyer/borrower makes payments.

The special warranty deed guarantees that during the time the buyer/borrower held equitable title to the property, one did nothing that would impede the title of the property.

If the buyer/borrower does not make payments and defaults on the property, the special warranty deed may be turned over to the seller/owner. The seller/owner presents an affidavit of default and the Escrow Agent turns over the seller/owner's warranty deed and the special warranty deed of the buyer/borrower. The seller/owner works with the Title Company to have legal title restored in the seller/owner's name.

If the buyer/borrower completes the Real Estate Contract according to terms, the Escrow Agent turns over the warranty deed and the special warranty deed to the buyer/borrower. It is the buyer/borrower's responsibility to have the seller/owner's warranty deed recorded and to shred the special warranty deed.

MEMORANDUM OF REAL ESTATE CONTRACT

A Memorandum of Real Estate Contract is an abbreviated document that may be filed with the County Clerk's Office, rather than filing the executed Real Estate Contract. The Memorandum of Real Estate Contract names the seller/owner and the buyer/borrower, lists the legal address of the property, and indicates there is a Real Estate Contract outstanding.

In my opinion, the option of using the Memorandum of Real Estate Contract is more attractive, since one may not want all of the information that is contained in the Real Estate Contract to become public information. The Memorandum of Real Estate Contract appeals to the contrarian in me, since I believe it is nobody's business to know the terms under which I am buying the property, such as its price or the monthly payment.

Next, we'll cover some different Real Estate Contract situations.

CHAPTER 7

REAL ESTATE CONTRACT SITUATIONS OVERVIEW

In this chapter, I provide an overview of how a Real Estate Contract (Contract) may be structured in different situations, and each party's possible responsibility and/or liability in each situation. We will review the instance in which there is no underlying mortgage, the instance in which the mortgage is assumed, and the instance in which the mortgage is "wrapped."

Although the parties to the Contract have the option of using an Escrow Agent as a conduit for payments, or of making payments directly, in all situations I recommend using the services of the Escrow Agent to handle the details of the Contract. It just makes for a smoother operation, as I will describe under each scenario.

Subsequent chapters will provide more detail of the possible situations or issues that may arise under the different scenarios.

PROPERTY WITH NO UNDERLYING MORTGAGE

When the seller/owner owns the property free and clear, there is little that need occupy the seller/owner's mind, except whether the buyer/borrower will complete the terms of the Contract. The Contract usually is very straightforward, and the buyer/borrower just needs to execute the terms of the Contract. This is one of the cleanest situations the parties to the Contract may encounter.

The only items about which the seller/owner need worry are whether the monthly payments are timely and the Contract amortizes (pays off the debt over the period of time at the interest rate indicated); and whether the buyer/borrower carries the appropriate insurance on the property and pays the property taxes. Regarding the amortization aspect, if the Contract does not amortize, it continues forever; and it may be unenforceable.

Upon entering into a Contract, the buyer/borrower should have the property assessed for taxation in one's name and provide that information to the Escrow Agent, assuming the Escrow Agent is collecting for taxes, to enable the Escrow Agent to pay the property taxes when due.

In addition, the buyer/borrower purchases hazard insurance to cover the structure, as well as liability insurance, and provides those details to the Escrow Agent. If there is a change in the amount due on the taxes and/or insurance, it is the buyer/borrower's responsibility to notify the Escrow Agent accordingly, if the Escrow Agent is collecting for taxes and insurance.

The hazard insurance should cover the seller/owner and buyer/borrower as their interest may appear in the property. Let's say, for example, the Contract is drawn up for $100,000.00, includes a single-family dwelling, and the buyer/borrower did not obtain the required property insurance. If the structure were to burn down and the buyer/borrower let the Contract go into default without curing the default, the seller/owner could get back an empty lot only worth $20,000.00.

If required by the Contract, the liability insurance for the property should name the seller/owner as an additional insured under the policy. There are several scenarios of how this may be accomplished; and this is where the services of a qualified insurance agent will come in, since it is the agent who will be called in the event of a claim. We will review those different insurance scenarios in a later chapter.

When drawing up the Contract, the principal and interest payment should be stated separately, with the dollar amount for the taxes and the insurance payment stated in another provision of the Contract. The prevailing thought is that it is easier for a buyer/borrower to pay 1/12 of the amount due for taxes and insurance with each payment, rather than to pay a larger amount for taxes and insurance on their respective due dates. This provision could provide some safety against the buyer/borrower going into default and protect the seller/owner.

The Escrow Agent (if one is being used) tracks the payments as they come in, and will not accept less than the required payment referenced in the Contract; i.e., the total payment required for the principal, interest, taxes, and insurances. In this way, the seller/owner is able to keep on top of the transaction and may intercede if an insurance payment or tax payment is not made in a timely fashion.

After the buyer/borrower completes the terms of the Contract, the Escrow Agent will release the deeds to the buyer/borrower. At this point, the buyer/borrower receives legal title to the property by filing the warranty deed at the County Clerk's Office.

Chapter 7

PROPERTY WITH AN ASSUMED MORTGAGE

When the seller/owner still has a mortgage on the property, it is possible the buyer/borrower may assume the existing mortgage, and also enter into a Real Estate Contract with the seller/owner. While mortgage assumption is an option, it may have limited application.

In Chapter 1, I discussed three common mortgage types: Conventional/conforming, FHA, and VA loans. As may be recalled, it was stated that FHA and VA loans generally may be assumed, providing the borrower meets qualification requirements. In this section, I describe the way in which assumed mortgages are handled in Real Estate Contract situations.

What Is An Assumed Mortgage?

Let's define what is meant by assumption. When a mortgage is assumed, it allows the individual to take over the mortgage at the same interest rate, the same term, and with the same unpaid principal balance as the original mortgage holder. The individual who assumes a mortgage pays the same monthly payment of principal and interest as the person who originated the loan. This means an individual assuming a 30-year mortgage after three years, will have 27 years left on the original mortgage.

For those of us who have been around the mortgage industry for a long period of time, it is not hard to understand the appeal of assuming a mortgage. For individuals who are unfamiliar with the mortgage industry or who are only familiar with today's low interest rates, a bit of historical perspective may be helpful.

Interest Rate History

In the late 1970s and early 1980s, interest rates rose to unbelievable heights. According to the Federal Deposit Insurance Corporation's Historical Timeline (found at FDIC.gov), mortgage interest rates reached a high of 21% in 1981. These high rates impacted the mortgage industry adversely.

At that time, mortgages were freely assumable. Rather than qualify for a mortgage with a high, double-digit interest rate, individuals preferred to assume a mortgage at a lower interest rate of say 10%, for example. Lenders, including banks and savings and loan associations, were placed at a disadvantage since they were forced to pay current interest rates to attract deposits, but were unable to obtain current interest rates on their mortgages when those mortgages were assumed. During the 1980s, many banks and savings and loan institutions failed.

The Remedy

As it is today, mortgages had a "due on sale" clause that allowed the lender to call the loan if the property were sold. This provision was originally intended to protect the lender's security interest from borrowers who assumed the mortgage, but were not creditworthy. During this period, lenders began enforcing the due on sale clause as a means to combat the interest rate disparity. Rather than allow the assumption of the loan, lenders called the loan, in order to lend money at the higher, prevailing interest rate.

It is noted that the due on sale clause was not enforced uniformly among the states nor among the lending institutions. Some states prohibited the enforcement of the due on sale clause, while others did not. During this time, assumption of mortgages continued. There were law suits regarding the enforcement of the due on sale clause, and one eventually reached the United States Supreme Court in 1982.

After the United States Supreme Court decision, Congress passed the Garn St. Germain Depository Institutions Act of 1982. This law effectively pre-empted any state statutes that prohibited the enforcement of the due on sale clause involving federal savings and loan associations, federal savings banks, federal credit unions, and national banks.

Note that the law also provided some exceptions in which the due on sale clause would not apply, such as transfer to a family member due to death of a borrower; or a transfer due to the death of a joint tenant; or the transfer due to a dissolution of marriage; just to name a few of the exceptions.

The provisions of the law became effective October 15, 1985, three years after the law was passed and limited the number of mortgages that were freely assumable. Although assumable mortgages were limited, they were still used with Real Estate Contracts, and the next section explains how.

Real Estate Contract With An Assumed Mortgage

If a seller/owner has a mortgage that may be assumed, a Real Estate Contract may be used for the seller/owner's equity in the property. This may be determined by subtracting the balance on the mortgage from the selling price of the property. The buyer/borrower agrees to pay the existing mortgage according to its terms, as well as the Real Estate Contract which represents the seller/owner's equity in the property. The existing mortgage and the balance due the seller/owner are both considered provisions of the Real Estate Contract, as far as the default provision is concerned.

Let's say a seller/owner has a property with a mortgage balance of $75,000.00, and sells the property for $150,000.00. After the buyer's down payment of $10,000.00, the parties execute a Contract for $65,000.00. This may be shown as follows:

Buyer/Borrower Will Pay	**$150,000.00**
Down Payment	**- $10,000.00**
Assumed Prior Obligations	**- $75,000.00**
Balance Due Seller/Owner	**=$65,000.00**

Buyer Will Assume First Mortgage of Seller and Will Also Execute a Real Estate Contract for $65,000.00

The seller/owner requests to be released from the obligation of the mortgage and asks the mortgage lender to substitute the buyer/borrower on the mortgage. When this is accomplished, the seller/owner no longer has an interest in the mortgage.

The buyer/borrower assumes the mortgage with the existing loan balance; the term; and the mortgage payment which generally includes principal, interest, taxes, and insurance. With the assumption of the mortgage, the property is assessed for taxation in the buyer/borrower's name. Note, that if the seller/owner is not released on the mortgage, the seller/owner remains liable for the mortgage.

A Real Estate Contract is drawn up for the balance due the seller/owner, noting the down payment, as well as the payment amount, the interest rate, and the terms of the payment. The Contract also states that the buyer/borrower shall maintain hazard insurance coverage for both the buyer/borrower and the seller/owner as their interests may appear, and may require liability insurance.

When an Escrow Agent is used for the payments, payment for the assumed mortgage and the Real Estate Contract is sent to an Escrow Agent who tracks the payments as they come in. The Escrow Agent forwards the appropriate amount to the mortgage lender and the balance according to the terms of the Contract.

Alternatively, when an Escrow Agent is not used, the buyer/borrower sends one payment to the mortgage lender for the assumed mortgage and another payment to the seller/owner for the Contract.

The Escrow Agent will not accept a partial payment of the total amount that is due, and that ensures the Contract operates according to terms. This prevents a scenario in which the buyer/borrower is making payments to the seller/owner, and not making payments on the assumed mortgage. By using an Escrow Agent, the seller/owner may be alerted before an assumed mortgage goes into foreclosure and may take preventive steps to protect one's interest.

After the buyer/borrower completes the terms of the Real Estate Contract, the seller/owner advises the Escrow Agent to release the warranty deed to the buyer/borrower. At this point, the buyer/borrower receives legal title to the property and must file the warranty deed at the County Clerk's Office. If the assumed mortgage is still outstanding, the legal title is subject to the mortgage.

PROPERTY WITH A "WRAPPED" MORTGAGE

If the seller/owner has a mortgage on the property that is not assumable, it is possible the seller/owner may "wrap" the existing mortgage, and enter into a Contract with a buyer/borrower. Wrapping a mortgage is an option, and both parties need to understand the responsibility and risk involved.

In the previous section, we discussed the "due on sale clause"; and this clause is germane to this section, as well. To restate, mortgages with a due on sale clause allow the mortgage lender to call or accelerate full payment of the unpaid balance due on the mortgage, if the borrower sells or disposes of the property. Using a Real Estate Contract with a wrapped mortgage is viewed as a way of trying to avoid the due on sale provision of an underlying mortgage.

With this scenario, the seller/owner has an outstanding mortgage that may not be assumed. The amount of the unpaid mortgage balance is added to the balance of the owner's equity in the property less the down payment, to achieve the Contract's amount. The buyer/borrower enters into the Contract with the seller/owner agreeing to make payments that will amortize the total amount of the Contract. The seller/owner generally uses this payment to cover the underlying mortgage to the lender and agrees to maintain the mortgage in good standing.

The Contract is structured so that the term of the Contract is at least as long as the term of the wrapped mortgage; and the payments are scheduled in such a way that allow the seller/owner's mortgage payment to be made in a timely manner. The underlying mortgage remains in the seller/owner's name. The pay-off of the mortgage coincides with the pay-off of the Real Estate Contract; and the seller/owner agrees to turn over the deed to the buyer/borrower when the Real Estate Contract is paid in full.

Since the Contract with a wrapped mortgage is executed to try to avoid the due on sale clause, the Contract should also contain a provision stating that the underlying mortgage may be called. If or when that happens, it is entirely the buyer/borrower's responsibility to make the payment of the total amount due. If the buyer/borrower fails to do so, it could be considered as defaulting on the Real Estate Contract.

Let's take the example used in the previous section to show how a Contract with a wrapped mortgage is structured. The seller/owner has a property with a mortgage balance of $75,000.00, and sells the property for $150,000.00. This unpaid mortgage balance of $75,000.00 is included in the Real Estate Contract. After the buyer's down payment of $10,000.00, the parties execute a Contract for $140,000.00. This may be shown as follows:

Buyer/Borrower Will Pay	$150,000.00
Down Payment	- $10,000.00
Assumed Prior Obligations	- $0.00
Balance Due Seller/Owner	=$140,000.00

Seller Wraps the First Mortgage; and Buyer and Seller Execute a Real Estate Contract for $140,000.00

When drawing up the Contract in this instance, the principal and interest payment are stated separately; and the dollar amount for the taxes and the insurance payment are also stated separately in the Contract, with the provision the amount may be adjusted as advised by the servicing company on the mortgage, or the Escrow Agent. Taxes and insurance are assumed to be paid through the first mortgage.

The Contract also states that the buyer/borrower shall maintain the appropriate hazard insurance coverage for the structure, as well as liability insurance for the property, if required. The mortgage lender and the seller/owner generally may be listed on this policy as loss payees.

If an Escrow Agent is being used, the buyer/borrower advises the Escrow Agent of the purchase of hazard insurance to cover the structure, as well as liability insurance (if required), and provides those details to the Escrow Agent. The premium for this insurance also becomes part of the Contract payment.

The payment under the Contract is sent to the Escrow Agent, who in turn, forwards the mortgage payment to the respective mortgage lender, and distributes the balance of the payment according to the terms of the Contract. If the parties do not use an Escrow Agent, the payment is sent to the seller/owner for appropriate distribution.

When using an Escrow Agent, the Escrow Agent keeps track of the payments as they come in, and will not accept a partial payment for the amount due. By using an Escrow Agent, the buyer/borrower is assured that payments to the wrapped mortgage are being made to the mortgage lender and not pocketed by the seller/owner.

After the buyer/borrower completes the term of the Contract, the Escrow Agent will release the deeds to the property. The buyer/borrower receives legal title and must file the warranty deed at the County Clerk's Office.

Why Use a Wrapped Mortgage?

As stated previously, a wrapped mortgage is an option that may be used with a Real Estate Contract. One may wonder why, if the lender may activate the due on sale clause, it is considered an alternative? In my opinion, there are a couple of reasons.

First of all, it allows a seller/owner who has a non-assumable mortgage outstanding and a buyer/borrower who wishes to purchase the property, the ability to enter into a Real Estate Contract for that property. When both the buyer/borrower and the seller/owner are knowledgeable regarding the risk involved (that the loan may be called), they can both plan for that contingency, accordingly. A problem arises when individuals enter into Real Estate Contracts without knowing the ramifications.

Secondly, it allows the seller/owner the possibility of making a spread on the interest rate between the underlying mortgage and the interest rate used in the Contract. If an underlying mortgage has an interest rate of 7%, and the Real Estate Contract has an interest rate of 8.5%, the seller/owner may make a spread (or gain) of 1.5% on the wrapped mortgage payment and a full 8.5% on the payment amount that represents the seller/owner's equity portion. In effect, the seller/owner uses the buyer/borrower's payment to earn interest, which may be an attractive feature to the seller/owner.

In this chapter, I have presented an overview of the provisions inherent in the different Real Estate Contract scenarios and how they are structured. In subsequent chapters, I discuss these provisions in detail

NOTE: The reader is strongly encouraged to consult an attorney before engaging in a "Wrap" contract or any other real estate investment.

CHAPTER 8

ANALYZING REAL ESTATE CONTRACT PROVISIONS

In Chapter 6, we looked at the components of a Real Estate Contract in general terms. In this and subsequent chapters, my goal is to discuss these provisions in detail and to identify any issues that may arise if these provisions are not addressed completely.

At this point, let me reiterate that I am not an attorney, nor do I give legal advice. I have been an Escrow Agent since 1987, and I have seen the issues that arise with poorly-drawn or improperly-drawn documents or incomplete documents.

Regardless of whether one is buying or selling under a Real Estate Contract, I encourage and recommend professionals and non-professionals alike to obtain the services of a Real Estate Professional, a Real Estate Attorney, a CPA (if applicable), a Title Company, and an Escrow Agent.

It is noted that a Real Estate Professional should be able to discuss the key provisions of a Real Estate Contract, but is unable to give advice regarding the way in which the provisions should be established. If there are any questions regarding the best way in which to establish the provisions, these questions should be referred to a Real Estate Attorney. After the buyer and seller come to an agreement on the provisions of the Contract, the Real Estate Attorney drafts the Real Estate Contract that the seller/owner and buyer/borrower eventually sign.

If the parties are working with a Realtor®, chances are the Realtor will use a current version of the Realtors® Association of New Mexico (RANM) Form which is an Addendum to Purchase Agreement-Real Estate Contract. This is a copy-written form that may be used only by Realtors.

In this chapter, we will cover the following provisions: name, the way in which the property is to be titled, and the property's address.

NAME

This is the way in which the seller/owner holds title to the property, and the way in which the buyer/borrower wishes to hold title to the property.

We all have nicknames by which we are addressed. We may be known by one name to our family and by another name to our friends. In the case of a Real Estate Contract, I recommend using an individual's legal name in this provision (where possible). This is an individual's official name and the one that is used in government documents, such as a social security card, passport, or driver's license. If title already resides in an individual wherein one has used a nickname, it is best, no doubt, to use this name in the Real Estate Contract since it appears on the title.

In the case of a business, the legal name of the business should be used. This is the name as it has been filed with the New Mexico Secretary of State.

TITLE

The name may be further modified by a phrase. For example, if the buyer/borrower or seller/owner is a single individual who has not been married, the name may be shown as follows:

"John Adams, a single man" or "Jane Adams, a single woman"

In the case of an individual who is legally divorced, the name may be shown:

"John Adams, an unmarried man" or "Jane Adams, an unmarried woman"

Then there is the case of a married individual who desires to acquire title as his/her separate property, and this may be shown:

"John Adams, a married man, as his sole and separate property" or

"Jane Adams, a married woman, as her sole and separate property"

Generally, in cases wherein married individuals want to hold title jointly, the names are shown as follows:

"John Adams and Jane Adams, husband and wife, as Joint Tenants"

In effect, this means the individuals hold the property jointly while both are alive, or individually after one of them dies. This is known as right of survivorship. If one of the joint tenants dies, the other joint tenant automatically receives that deceased joint tenant's ownership interest. It is easy to understand in a husband and wife situation; if husband John dies, wife Jane receives John's interest in the property, and vice versa.

There is also another joint tenant arrangement, and this is called Tenants In Common. In this arrangement, the tenants own what is called undivided interests in the property. This means title may be held with unequal ownership shares, and at the death of one of the joint tenants, that respective ownership share goes to the deceased joint tenant's estate and is distributed according to the terms of the will.

For example, John Adams and Fred Smith who are business associates could hold title as unequal owners. Let's say that John Adams owns a 40% interest and Fred Smith owns a 60% interest. Title may be shown as follows:

"John Adams, a married man, as his sole and separate property, as to an undivided 2/5ths interest, and Fred Smith, an unmarried man, as to an undivided 3/5ths interest as Tenants in Common."

With this Tenants in Common arrangement, if Fred were to die, his undivided 3/5ths interest in the property would not go to John, but would go to Fred's estate. The property interest would then be distributed according to the terms of Fred's will. John's undivided 2/5ths interest in the property would not be impacted in any way.

There are situations wherein property may be owned by other than an individual. This may apply if a corporation, partnership, or limited liability company is purchasing the property. In that case, the company's name would be shown, such as "New Mexico's Finest, LLC."

Then there is another instance with a Self-Directed IRA. Real estate is a popular investment for Self-Directed IRAs,

Chapter 8

and it is often purchased by way of a Real Estate Contract. In this instance, the Custodian for the Self-Directed IRA is the buyer for the IRA, and title would be shown as "Sunwest Trust, Custodian for John Adams Self-Directed IRA."

LEGAL ADDRESS

This is the address of the property that is the subject of the Real Estate Contract, and the legal description for the property as it appears on the deed is used here. The legal description of the property includes the boundaries of the property. It is used so that a surveyor would be able to identify the property. The legal description should include the county and the municipality in which the property is located.

There are several different methods that may be used to measure the property. One method uses "metes and bounds." It is based generally upon using a natural monument such as a tree or rock outcrop as a starting point, and following a course around the property that is designated by direction and degrees.

Property may be described using the Government Survey System which could include the following words: township, section, baselines, and Principal Meridians.

Then there is the subdivision plat that is a map of a subdivision that is approved and recorded by the county in which the property is located; it shows the subdivision lots and street names. The legal description includes the subdivision name, lot number, and the book and page number of the county's records. The following is an example of a legal address using this method:

Lots 34, 35 and 36 in San Miguel Acres, a subdivision of a tract of land in the Southwest Quarter of Section 18, T9N, R6E, N.M.P.M., Bernalillo County and State of New Mexico, as the same is shown and designated on the plat thereof filed in the Office of the County Clerk and Ex-Officio Recorder of Bernalillo County and State of New Mexico on the 8th day of December, 1953.

TOGETHER WITH any and all improvements on the above-described property.

STREET ADDRESS

Note that the street address is necessary to locate the property, but it is not known as the legal description.

The street address used in the Real Estate Contract is the street address of the subject property, and this is a key area for focus. In addition to giving the street address for the property being purchased, it is important to give what is called a "default address." This is the address to which a demand letter will be sent, in case the buyer/borrower defaults on the Contract.

Let's say a seller/owner and buyer/borrower enter into a Real Estate Contract for a piece of property, and the property's street address is listed in the Real Estate Contract, along with the legal description. If the buyer/borrower moves in and is living at this street address, that is all very well and good. The seller/owner knows where to advise one's attorney to mail documents to the buyer/borrower in case a situation of default ever arises. This gives the buyer/borrower notice that there is a default situation and the time and ability to cure the default, if one so desires.

Chapter 8

Assuming the same Real Estate Contract previously described, let's say the buyer/borrower does not move in, but uses the property as a rental and lives elsewhere. If the buyer/borrower defaults on the Real Estate Contract, the demand letter to cure the default is sent to the address on the Real Estate Contract.

As a point of information, demand letters generally are required to be sent certified mail with a return receipt requested, as well as regular mail. Chances are the renter may ignore the notice of certified mail, and also may ignore the letter sent by regular mail. This could produce a situation wherein the buyer/borrower does not cure the default in time and subsequently loses the property.

Terry Tip:
Sunwest Escrow had this exact situation happen sometime ago with one of its escrow accounts. As the Escrow Agent handling this Real Estate Contract, we had the buyer's address as noted on the Real Estate Contract. The Contract went into default, and the seller/owner had his attorney send a demand letter to the property address.

Unfortunately, the buyer/borrower did not receive the demand letter since he had rented out the property referenced in the Contract. Hence, he did not cure the default in the stated period of time and the property went back to the seller/owner.

As a first reaction, we may feel sorry for the buyer/borrower since he lost the property due to this oversight. However, he was charging and receiving a rent payment from the occupant living at the property, but was not sending his Real Estate Contract payment to the Escrow Agent. This was a violation of the terms of the Real Estate Contract he signed. Actions (or inactions in this case) have consequences.

Another Terry Tip:
Avoid a costly mistake. When completing the information for a Real Estate Contract, one is required to use the property address which is the subject of the Contract. In addition, one should always give a "default address" to avoid the foregoing situation from happening.

In the property address section of the document, one can indicate that the property address is the default address. If that is not the case, in the section of the document for other information, one can indicate the default address, if it is different from the property address.

In the next chapter, we cover the price and payment section of the Real Estate Contract.

CHAPTER 9

PRICE AND PAYMENT

Generally, the next section of a Real Estate Contract focuses on the total price the buyer/borrower is paying for the real property, the payment that is due, how the payment is to be applied to the balance due the seller/owner, and the late charge and collection provision of the contract.

In the next two chapters, we will go into great detail, because it is important to understand these provisions in their entirety.

BUYER WILL PAY

The total price is restated and comprises the down payment; any assumed prior obligations, such as a mortgage if applicable; and the equity owed the seller/owner. (Please refer to Chapter 7 for a review of what is meant by an assumed mortgage or a wrapped mortgage.)

As far as the down payment is concerned, this is the amount paid to the seller/owner and to which the seller/owner has immediate access. It is not the earnest money that has been paid to bind the purchase agreement to show the buyer/borrower's legitimate interest in the property; but note, the down payment could include the dollar amount of any earnest money that has already been paid and is held in escrow, if the parties agree to this.

Just Another Tool...

Let's review a couple of examples:

Example One
The seller/owner could own the property free and clear or there could be a first mortgage outstanding that the seller/owner is wrapping in the Real Estate Contract. In this instance:

Buyer Will Pay	$100,000.00
Down Payment	$10,000.00
Assumed Prior Obligations	$0.00
Balance Due Seller	$90,000.00

In Example One, $90,000.00 is the amount the seller/owner is financing over the term of the Real Estate Contract.

Example Two
The seller/owner has a first mortgage and the buyer/borrower is going to assume that first mortgage and execute a Real Estate Contract for the balance due on the property. In this instance:

Buyer Will Pay	$100,000.00
Down Payment	$10,000.00
Assumed Prior Obligations	$50,000.00
Balance Due Seller	$40,000.00

In Example Two, $40,000.00 is the amount the seller/owner is financing over the term of the Real Estate Contract.

Chapter 9

PAYABLE AS FOLLOWS

After the dollar amount of the Real Estate Contract is determined, it is necessary to state the details of how the loan will be financed over the term of the Contract. This section identifies the date the payment is due, the date on which interest begins to accrue, the interest rate used to amortize the Contract, and the term of the Contract.

There also may be the provision that the payments will be made to an Escrow Agent whose name appears in the Contract. From an Escrow Agent's point of view, the payable as follows provision is the most important provision of the Contract, since this provides direction to the Escrow Agent in the way payments should be disbursed.

The following is an example of a Payable as Follows provision for a Real Estate Contract for $10,000.00:

"$10,000.00 is the amount of this Real Estate Contract, which purchasers agree to pay in monthly installments of $200.00 each or more, including interest at 5%, from October 6, 2014, with like installments due and payable on the 6th day of each succeeding month thereafter until November 6, 2019, at which time the entire remaining balance, including any and all accrued interest, shall be due and payable in full."

In this example, the amount of the monthly payment is $200.00 and the first payment is due on October 6, 2014. The subsequent due dates for the payment are likewise due on the "6th" of each month following. The interest rate charged is 5%. The term of the Contract is for 60 months or five years. At the end of this period, there is a balloon payment due for the balance and any and all accrued interest.

Let's further break down this *payable as follows* paragraph to analyze and identify possible problem areas.

PRINCIPAL AND INTEREST ONLY

A Real Estate Contract "unbundles" the payment that is required by the buyer/borrower. For example, when most individuals discuss their mortgage payment, they generally state a monthly dollar amount; this dollar amount generally includes principal, interest, property taxes, and insurance.

The industry term for this is *PITI*, signifying principal, interest, taxes, and insurance. Of this payment, the principal and interest charge remains level over the term of the mortgage. The property taxes and insurance component of the payment can fluctuate or change.

When property taxes increase or there is a shortage of escrow for insurance and taxes, the individual who is the borrower receives a notice from the mortgage servicer (or the Escrow Agent if there isn't a first mortgage) that the monthly payment will increase. It is not the principal and interest component of the payment that increases, but the property taxes and/or insurance component that increases.

In the price and payment section of the Real Estate Contract, the principal and interest amount is stated separately. The taxes and insurance portions of the payment are stated in another provision.

This is an important difference to keep in mind. First of all, it is necessary to include the taxes and insurance components in the Contract; and secondly, it is important for the parties (either the seller/owner or the buyer/borrower) to advise the Escrow Agent when an increase or decrease occurs.

Further, the interest rate can be any rate agreed upon by the seller/owner and the buyer/borrower. To my knowledge, there are no usury laws in the state of New Mexico. It has been my experience to see rates as high as 21% and as low as zero. As a rule of thumb, it probably is possible to charge an interest rate that is 3.5% to 4% above the mortgage interest rate for an owner-occupied home.

Terry Tip:
Although I have seen 0% interest charged on a Real Estate Contract over the course of my experience, I would not recommend that this be done by the seller/owner. The Internal Revenue Code (IRC) has a section which pertains to below-market loans (IRC Section 7872). In effect, if a seller/owner charges an interest rate that is below market according to the IRC, the seller/owner may receive *imputed interest income* which must be declared on one's income tax return.

The Applicable Federal Rates (AFR) are published monthly and a seller/owner would be wise to consult with one's attorney or accountant before charging a below-market rate on a Real Estate Contract.

Another Terry Tip:
Let me say a word about agreeing to a rate or negotiating a rate. If I offer a Real Estate Contract at 7%, for example, and the potential buyer doesn't want to pay 7%, but offers to pay 5%, I have a decision to make. The decision is whether to agree to the 5% or to engage in further negotiation to get to my original rate. In any event, the rate in the Contract will be the rate agreed upon by both parties.

MONTHLY INSTALLMENTS OF $200.00 OR MORE

The payment described in a Real Estate Contract is stated as the "dollar amount due or more," as in our example $200.00 or more. It is my understanding that in New Mexico a prepayment penalty cannot be enforced on a residential mortgage; and if the Contract were written so that the payment was limited to only a certain amount (in our example $200.00), this could be construed as a prepayment penalty.

In effect, if the buyer/borrower wished to pay $200.00 or $400.00 or even $800.00 per month, the Escrow Agent would accept that amount. Note, that an Escrow Agent is unable to accept any amount less than the amount stated in the Real Estate Contract, however.

Terry Tip:
Invariably, whenever I teach the contents of this book as continuing education for real estate professionals and others, the comment arises that they or one of their clients has employed a prepayment penalty in a residential Real Estate Contract.

For example, a seller/owner may have the Real Estate Contract written so that the buyer/borrower is charged a $5,000.00 penalty in the event the buyer/borrower pays off the Contract early. If the buyer/borrower were to pay the balance due, early and in full, without the prepayment penalty amount, the seller/owner would need to sue the buyer/borrower to enforce this provision in order to receive the penalty amount.

Although I am not an attorney, it is my understanding this provision is not enforceable on a residential loan; and in my opinion, if a seller/owner tried to enforce this provision by suing the buyer/borrower, the suit may not be successful.

This is yet another reason to employ the services of a Real Estate Attorney when drafting a Real Estate Contract.

PAYMENT DUE ON THE 6TH DAY OF EACH MONTH

Traditionally, we expect a mortgage payment to be due on the first of each month, and that is generally the practice with mortgage lenders. In a Real Estate Contract however, any due date is viable; and the seller/owner and the buyer/borrower can agree to any date during the month. In this example, we have used the 6th as the due date.

When contemplating a payment due date, it is necessary to determine if the Contract contains a wrapped mortgage, since this may have some bearing on the payment due date. In a wrap situation, the underlying mortgage usually is paid with the money received from the Real Estate Contract payment; typically, the Escrow Agent is instructed to pay the underlying mortgage, and then forward any additional amount to the seller/owner.

Since mortgages are generally due on the first of the month, an optimal payment due date for the Wrap Real Estate Contract would be a week or two before the payment is due on the underlying mortgage. This enables the Escrow Agent to ensure the underlying mortgage payment arrives in a timely manner.

Terry Tip:
Remember, if the buyer/borrower under a Real Estate Contract does not pay on time, the seller/owner may be forced to pay the underlying wrapped mortgage out of pocket. Further, it is the seller/owner's credit history that is

on the line, if there are late payments or missed payments in a wrap Contract situation.

A seller/owner should consider making a payment at least one month ahead on the wrapped mortgage. With this approach, the seller/owner will have a 30-day leeway, in case the buyer/borrower does not make the Real Estate Contract payment. With today's technology, it is easier for the seller/owner to monitor the status of the wrapped mortgage.

WHEN DOES INTEREST START?

It may be assumed that interest is charged beginning with the date the Contract is executed, but this may not be the case. One of the parties to the Contract may live out of state and it would be impossible for both parties to execute the contract on the same date. Or, if that were not the case, the seller/owner simply may be agreeable to defer charging interest for a few days.

There is no law stating that interest is required to be charged immediately. Take, for instance, our foregoing example wherein interest accrues from the 6th of October. If the Contract were executed on September 25th, this would be a case of the seller/owner foregoing the interest for a period of days; and this could be done.

In the next chapter, we will discuss the way in which interest is credited, and amortization issues.

CHAPTER 10

INTEREST CREDITING AND AMORTIZATION

Continuing with the Real Estate Contract provisions, we will discuss how the payment is applied to the balance due the seller/owner, and the late charge and collection provision of the Contract.

WILL THE CONTRACT AMORTIZE?

It is important to ascertain that the payment, along with the interest rate factor, will pay off the loan amount over the period identified. This is called amortization.

Nowadays, we generally do not see Real Estate Contracts that do not amortize over the term of the loan; but I have seen them in my career experience as an Escrow Agent and as a buyer of Real Estate Contracts.

If the Contract does not amortize, the loan will never be repaid; moreover, the interest which is accruing could add to the balance due the seller/owner. Allow me to share this experience.

Some time ago, I purchased a Real Estate Contract that was about five or six years into its term; I bought it at a discount. Very quickly I discovered that the Contract did not amortize.

The Contract was for $36,000.00, the interest rate was 9%, and the buyer/borrower was paying $200.00 per month.

After doing the calculation, I determined the monthly cost of interest alone on this Contract was $270.00. Not only did the Contract not amortize, the monthly payment was not enough to pay the interest on the Contract, and there was accrued unpaid interest of $4,000.00 due. The balance of the Contract was still $36,000.00. Apparently there was confusion by both parties when the Contract was drawn up regarding how a Real Estate Contract should operate.

After doing some calculations, I offered to reduce the interest rate to 4%, if the buyer/borrower would increase the payment to $500.00. In this way, the buyer/borrower would pay down the principal; the Contract could amortize; and the buyer/borrower would eventually own the property. Unfortunately, the buyer/borrower only spoke Spanish; so I communicated the situation and the solution to her granddaughter who spoke English.

I am unclear whether the issue here was communicated correctly or even understood. In any event, the buyer/borrower did not take advantage of this offer and continued paying only $200.00 per month on the Contract, and continued accumulating accrued unpaid interest.

Some two years later, the granddaughter advised me her grandmother (the buyer/borrower) was moving back to Mexico and wanted to give the property back to me. Since the property had appreciated, I suggested that her grandmother try to sell the property as a means of recouping some of the money that she had put into payments.

Ultimately, the next door neighbor bought the Contract from her (I am unaware of the terms) and took over the payments. Since the neighbor understood the basics of the Contract, he started paying $500.00 per month, but at the 9% interest rate. Sometimes, he has made two payments per month, and now the balance on this Contract is reduced to about $15,000.00.

FIGURING PAYMENTS

With technology advances, there is no reason for this situation to occur. When I started in the business, it was necessary to calculate amortization schedules manually by using a book with tables of interest factors and periods of time; these were called Ellwood Tables. If one did not align the correct interest factor and period of time, this could result in an inaccurate amortization schedule.

From manual calculations, the industry moved to hand-held calculators that specialized in complex financial functions; and now, it is possible to download an application that will perform complex financial functions to a smartphone.

Depending on the type of calculator being used, these are the following keys that are used for the components of a Real Estate Contract:

N equals the term of the Contract or the total number of payments. Since calculations are usually done on a monthly basis, one needs to remember to convert years to months, such as 10 years to 120 months or 15 years to 180 months, for example.

I equals the interest rate stated in the Contract; it is also entered as a monthly rate.

PV is the present value and it is the amount of the Contract.

PMT is the amount of the monthly payment. Remember that this is principal and interest only. Note that on most Hewlett Packard (HP®) calculators, the payment must be entered as a negative number. Taxes and insurance will be stated in the Contract in another provision.

FV is another key that is often used and it is used in determining the value for a future balloon payment, after several years' payments have been made.

Note that Real Estate Contract calculations may be performed based upon four variable components. If one knows three out of the four variable components, one is able to solve for the fourth component.

Terry Tip:
I want to say a word regarding balloon payments. As previously stated, a seller/owner may charge a higher interest rate on a Real Estate Contract than a buyer/borrower may obtain through qualifying for a mortgage. In some instances, a buyer/borrower is encouraged to enter into a Real Estate Contract for a short period and then to pay off the Contract with a balloon payment. It is assumed the buyer/borrower will work on one's ability to qualify for a mortgage during this time.

Be wary of Contracts with short terms until the balloon payment is due. In my opinion, a seller/owner is setting oneself up for a re-negotiation of the Contract if the balloon payment is any sooner than five years. An individual with a poor credit history does not change one's payment habits overnight; it may take a period of years.

Chapter 10

APPLICATION OF THE PAYMENTS TO THE BALANCE

One of the provisions in this section pertains to the way in which the Real Estate Contract payments are credited to the interest due, and the way in which interest is calculated; this impacts the payment that is ultimately applied to the balance due to the seller/owner. The parties to the Contract decide whether to use periodic interest or daily interest.

Periodic Interest assumes a 30-day period between each monthly payment. In effect, 12 months of 30 days each makes a 360-day year. Periodic interest assumes that the payments are made when due, regardless of when the payment comes in; and every payment is assumed to be made on the 1st of the month.

Daily Interest works on a 365-day year (except when there is a Leap year and there are 366 days) and accumulates the interest from the date of the last payment until such time as when the next payment is received. When a payment is not made on its respective due date, the daily interest begins to accrue and this may have unintended consequences. A daily interest rate often is used in Real Estate Contracts.

Example With Periodic Interest

The best way to show the difference in the application of interest is to provide examples of each. Let's assume a Real Estate Contract with a payment due date of the 1st. In this example, the buyer/borrower plans to be out of the country for a couple of months and wants to make payments to cover the loan while away. The last payment was made on February 1st; and it is now March 3rd. The buyer/borrower wants to make the payment due on March 1st and April 1st,

89

and will be back in time to make the May 1st payment. The buyer/borrower pays an amount equal to two payments on March 3rd.

Under the Contract using periodic interest, the amount is applied as if the payments came in on the date they were due, and 30 days' interest is credited on the payment for March, and on the payment for April; the rest of the payment is applied to the balance due the seller/owner. On May 1st, the buyer/borrower makes the next payment.

Example With Daily Interest

Under the Contract using daily interest, the amount equal to two payments is applied on the day it came in, March 3rd. The number of days since the last payment was made on February 1 is calculated. February 2 to February 29 (since this is a Leap year) is 28 days. It is now March 3, so that adds 3 more days. In effect, 31 days' interest (28 days + 3 days) are credited and the rest of the payment is applied to the balance due the seller/owner, with the next due date being May 1st.

On May 1st, the buyer/borrower makes a payment and this payment is credited to the interest that has accrued since March 3, the date of the last payment. There are 28 days' interest from March, and 30 days' interest from April, and one day's interest from May, making a total of 59 days' interest (28 days + 30 days + 1 day =59 days) that are credited from the May 1st payment, before any amount may be applied to the balance due the seller/owner.

In this daily interest example, let's say the monthly payment is $100.00, and let's further state that when the buyer/borrower makes the May 1st payment, the amount of accrued interest due for the 59 days is $150.00. The May 1ˢᵗ payment would have the $100.00 credited toward accrued interest; $50.00 accrued unpaid interest would remain; and nothing would go toward the balance due the seller/owner.

In effect, each subsequent payment is used to reduce the accrued unpaid interest, then toward paying the accrued interest, until if any of the payment is left over, it is used toward the principal balance due the seller/owner.

In the foregoing example, even though the buyer/borrower made what one thought were two payments with daily interest, interest was calculated from the last payment on March 3ʳᵈ until the next payment was made on May 1ˢᵗ. The balance of the March 3ʳᵈ payment went to reduce the principal or the balance due the seller/owner. This created an accrued unpaid interest situation.

Note, if the buyer/borrower gets far enough behind on the accrued unpaid interest, it can extend the term of the loan.

Terry Tip:
I want to share a couple of experiences I've had with interest payments and buyers. The first experience involves a buyer/borrower with whom I have a Real Estate Contract for a property outside Albuquerque. The Contract is written with a periodic interest rate which means it assumes 12 periods of 30 days' interest. This buyer/borrower had not made a payment in over a year, but recently started making payments again. Recently, he just made his January 2015 payment. Although I haven't had a payment in over a year, only 30 days' interest was applied in that payment.

There is another experience with a buyer/borrower with whom I have a Real Estate Contract, and this Contract is written with daily interest or a 365-day year. Interest accrues from the date of the last payment. This borrower missed six payments, so now is faced with the situation where every one of the payments goes to accrued unpaid interest. With this pattern, it may be a couple of years before any payment could be used toward the balance due seller.

LATE CHARGES AND COLLECTION COSTS

As with any provision in a Real Estate Contract, the terms of the Contract are negotiable, and require the agreement of both parties.

Generally speaking, after establishing the payment amount, interest rate, and the due date of the payment; a provision is inserted notifying the buyer/borrower the amount of any late charge. The Contract states the number of days that must elapse after a payment due date, before a late charge is assessed. The dollar amount of the late charge is stated, as well as the fact that the buyer/borrower is responsible for paying this late charge.

The number of days and the late charge amount are agreed upon by both parties. Note that individuals' perceptions generally align with any experience they may have had with mortgages. Individuals are generally familiar with payments due on the 1st, and with late payments being charged after the 15th. In a Real Estate Contract, there could be a late charge that becomes due when the payment is 10 days overdue, for example.

For instance, in the previous chapter's example wherein $200.00 was due on October 6, and each installment was due on the 6th in subsequent months, the seller/owner could assess a late charge on the 17th of the month, if one were inclined to do so.

It is important to bear in mind that the number of days until a late charge is assessed is different from the determination of when a payment is late. A payment is late on the next day following the payment due date, because the Contract clearly states the date on which payment is due. The period of time wherein a payment is due and a late charge is assessed is not a grace period.

In the example of the payment due on the 6th, the payment is late on the 7th, and the Contract is in default. According to the Contract provisions, a demand letter to cure the default of the Contract could be sent by the seller/owner's attorney on the 7th of the month.

Terry Tip:
I share the story of a seller/owner who became very frustrated because he was a party to a Real Estate Contract with a buyer/borrower who consistently made his payment on the 10th of the month to avoid paying a late fee on the 11th. The seller/owner lost 10 days' interest each month, and solicited my advice regarding how to handle this issue. I advised him of the option of sending the demand letter on the day after the payment was due. The seller/owner consulted his attorney and decided to send the demand letter on the 2nd.

As may be expected, the buyer/borrower called to tell us we had made a mistake and the seller/owner had no right to authorize a demand letter to be sent. We advised him to the contrary; the buyer/borrower cured the default; and as far as I know, the buyer/borrower is making his payments on time.

Just Another Tool...

In the next chapter we discuss other payments, such as taxes and insurance and assumed prior obligations.

CHAPTER 11

INSURANCE, PRIOR OBLIGATIONS & TAXES

In the last chapter we discussed interest crediting, amortization, and late charges. In this chapter, we discuss the payments for taxes, insurance, and prior obligations that are described in the Real Estate Contract. We will review the benefits for each party when these payments are made through an Escrow Agent.

A Real Estate Contract identifies and shows any assumed prior obligations and outlines the way in which payments for these prior obligations will be made by the party responsible for them.

In addition, a Real Estate Contract requires that the buyer/borrower maintain insurance for the benefit of the buyer and the seller as their interests may appear. The seller/owner needs to ascertain that the coverage is in force and is satisfactory. There is always the possibility of default by the buyer/borrower and that the seller/owner will get the property back. This is why the seller/owner has an interest in the insurance.

Hazard insurance is placed on the property to cover any structural damage to the property. There may be public liability insurance, as well, to cover incidents that may occur on the property, such as an individual falling and breaking one's leg and suing both parties.

Generally, the hazard insurance is shown as a stated amount or the amount may be defined as a formula. The way in which the insurance is arranged is dependent on whether there is an underlying mortgage. The public liability insurance is stated as a dollar amount with the seller/owner named as an additional insured.

Let's take a look at the different situations.

PROPERTY OWNED FREE AND CLEAR

When the seller/owner owns the property free and clear, there is no mortgage or lien outstanding on the property, and no prior obligations. After the Real Estate Contract is executed, the buyer/borrower has the County Clerk record the Real Estate Contract or Memorandum of Real Estate Contract in the buyer/borrower's name. In this way, tax notices are sent directly to the buyer/borrower.

Since there is no mortgage, the buyer/borrower purchases a Homeowner's policy, and names the seller/owner as a lienholder on the policy. In addition, the buyer/borrower may be asked to maintain public liability insurance with the seller/owner named as an additional insured on the liability policy.

The Real Estate Contract generally requires that the buyer/borrower provide the seller/owner annual proof of both insurances, as well as proof of the payment of taxes. There are two ways to handle the insurance and tax provision.

Chapter 11

Payments

The buyer/borrower may send the principal and interest payment to the Escrow Agent, and pay the taxes and insurance directly; or the buyer/borrower may send the principal and interest payment, as well as the payment for taxes and insurances to the Escrow Agent for proper distribution. Regardless of the option agreed upon, it is stated in the Real Estate Contract.

If the buyer/borrower sends the payments for the taxes and insurances directly, the seller/owner loses control of the situation since there is no way of knowing whether these payments have been paid, unless the seller/owner asks for proof.

If the buyer/borrower makes the payments of taxes and insurances in periodic payments, along with each periodic payment of principal and interest to the Escrow Agent, both parties gain.

The buyer/borrower may break down the payment of taxes and insurance into manageable amounts, and the Escrow Agent will disburse those additional monies to pay the taxes and insurances as due. The seller/owner stays on top of the situation and is aware immediately if any payment has not been made, since the Escrow Agent is not allowed to accept any amount less than what is stated in the Real Estate Contract. This ensures less chance of Contract default.

Note, it is the respective party's responsibility to advise the Escrow Agent of any changes in the insurance premiums or tax bill, and it is also the respective party's obligation to present the bills to the Escrow Agent for payment. It is not the Escrow Agent's responsibility to know if there has been a change.

ASSUMED MORTGAGE

In this situation, the buyer/borrower takes over the seller/owner's existing mortgage with the existing loan balance, the term, and the mortgage payment which includes principal and interest. The buyer/borrower assumes the mortgage through a qualification process with the existing mortgage lender.

The assumption of a mortgage is characterized and listed as a prior obligation in the Real Estate Contract, and an assumed mortgage is viewed as an addendum to the Real Estate Contract. This means that if the buyer/borrower does not comply with the terms of the assumed mortgage or the terms of the Real Estate Contract, the Contract goes into default.

With the assumption of the mortgage, the property should be assessed for taxation in the buyer/borrower's name. Mortgage lenders always require hazard insurance on the property to which the buyer/borrower must comply.

This dovetails nicely with the Real Estate Contract, since the Real Estate Contract requires the buyer/borrower to maintain hazard insurance coverage for both the buyer and the seller as their interests may appear, and may require liability insurance.

The buyer/borrower purchases a Homeowner's policy, and names the seller/owner as a lienholder on the policy. The premium for this hazard policy which is the requirement of the mortgage lender and of the Contract, is included as part of the mortgage payment that is sent to the mortgage lender or mortgage servicer.

Since the assumed mortgage payment sent to the mortgage lender or mortgage servicer comprises principal, interest, taxes, and hazard insurance, the provision in the Contract that states the buyer/borrower pay the taxes is also satisfied.

Irrespective of the assumed mortgage, the seller/owner may require the buyer/borrower to purchase a liability policy that names the seller/owner as an additional insured.

Payments

In the assumed mortgage situation, as with the previous situation described, the buyer/borrower may send the mortgage payment and the payment for the liability insurance directly to the respective mortgage servicer or lender and the insurance company. As an alternative, the buyer/borrower may send the mortgage payment and the liability insurance payment to the Escrow Agent, along with the principal and interest payment for the Contract. The way in which the payment for the insurance and prior obligations is handled is stated in the Real Estate Contract.

Again, if the buyer/borrower sends the payments for the prior obligation directly, the seller/owner may lose control of the situation. The buyer/borrower may send the Contract payment to the Escrow Agent and not send the payment for the assumed mortgage to the mortgage lender or servicer. This could create a foreclosure situation of which the seller/owner is not aware.

By using the Escrow Agent, payments are tracked as they come in and are forwarded in the appropriate amount to the mortgage lender or servicer, the liability insurer, and the seller/owner according to the terms of the Contract.

The Escrow Agent will not accept a partial payment of the total amount that is due, and that ensures the Contract operates according to terms. This prevents a scenario in which the buyer/borrower is making payments to the seller/owner, and not making payments on the assumed mortgage. By using an Escrow Agent, the seller/owner may be alerted before an assumed mortgage goes into foreclosure and take preventive steps to protect one's interest.

Note, it is the buyer/borrower's responsibility to advise the Escrow Agent of any changes in the mortgage payment (due to taxes or insurance) or liability insurance premium.

WRAPPED MORTGAGE

Disclaimer: Author is not recommending or approving the use of a Wrap Real Estate Contract. The parties involved must understand the complications involved with a Wrap and are strongly advised to seek legal counsel.

In the Real Estate Contract with a wrapped mortgage, the mortgage stays under the seller/owner's name. The buyer/borrower makes a payment under the Contract that is large enough to cover the principal and interest payment due on the underlying mortgage, as well as the principal and interest payment to cover the portion that is financed under the Real Estate Contract.

The buyer/borrower is required to pay the taxes and obtain hazard insurance, and could be required to purchase a public liability insurance policy naming the seller/owner as an additional insured.

Unlike the two previous examples regarding the hazard insurance, there is not an easy answer of the way in which the insurance should be handled on a Wrap Real Estate Contract. As a point of information, there are three options that are discussed for insurance and they are presented.

Option 1:
Under this option, the seller/owner maintains the original insurance policy on the property that comprises part of the monthly payment to the mortgage lender or mortgage servicer. The buyer/borrower obtains a homeowner's policy on the property according to the terms of the Real Estate Contract.

There is a possible issue here since in effect, the seller/owner is no longer the homeowner. In addition, there are two hazard insurance policies on the property. If there were a claim there would be two homeowners' policies. The insurance company for the seller/owner may say that it is the buyer/borrower's problem, and vice versa. Although this option has been used for many years, it appears this option may have some issues.

Option 2
Under this option, the seller/owner makes the request of one's property insurance agent to add the buyer/borrower as an additional insured on the seller/owner's original homeowner's policy. This may appear to the mortgage lender as a situation in which the buyer/borrower has loaned money to the original insured.

At issue here is that the seller/owner no longer owns the property, but is listed in the homeowner's policy as the homeowner. If there were a loss, the claim may not cover the buyer/borrower's belongings. Further, in case of a loss, the claim proceeds check may be paid only to the seller/owner as the homeowner, or may be made payable to both of them. It would seem that both parties may have an issue with getting the insurance proceeds disbursed properly so that repairs could be made on the property.

Option 3
In the last option, the seller/owner instructs the property insurance agent to change the homeowner's policy into a landlord's policy or a fire policy. The buyer/borrower would be instructed to obtain a renter's policy for the contents of the structure.

In this way, if there were a fire, the landlord's policy would cover the structure and the renter's policy would cover the contents of the structure. In effect, two separate claims would be made on two separate policies for two separate insureds.

In my research over the last several years regarding how the hazard insurance should be arranged on a Real Estate Contract with a wrapped mortgage, it has been the consensus of several property insurance agents that Option 3 is generally recommended.

Terry Tip:
When selling a piece of property with a wrapped mortgage, I recommend engaging the services of one's property insurance agent and explaining the terms of the Real Estate Contract to the agent, to see what the agent would recommend. After all, if there were a claim, it is the property insurance agent who will represent the seller/owner in the claim.

Chapter 11

Payments

The wrapped mortgage is listed and described in the Real Estate Contract as a prior obligation and the Real Estate Contract outlines the way in which the prior obligations will be handled. Since the wrapped mortgage is still in the seller/owner's name, the seller/owner may pay it directly to the mortgage lender or mortgage servicer or may pay it through an Escrow Agent.

Rather than relying on the seller/owner to pay the wrapped mortgage directly, it is recommended that all payments be routed through an Escrow Agent. The buyer/borrower makes principal and interest payment, plus taxes and insurance, as well as the payment for the liability insurance if applicable, as payment on the Real Estate Contract to the Escrow Agent. The Escrow Agent forwards the wrapped mortgage payment of principal, interest, taxes, and insurance to the mortgage lender or mortgage servicer, applies principal and interest payment to the balance due the seller/owner, and pays the premium for the public liability insurance. Any amount left over is then distributed to the seller/owner.

In this way, the buyer knows that the part of the payment allocated to the wrapped mortgage is actually going to the mortgage lender or mortgage servicer, and that the wrapped mortgage is being paid, along with the principal and interest due the seller/owner on the Real Estate Contract.

The advantage to the seller/owner is the knowledge that the Escrow Agent will not accept any payment that is less than the amount that is stated in the Contract; this ensures that the Real Estate Contract operates according to its terms. If the seller/owner receives one's monthly payment, the seller/owner knows that the wrapped mortgage has been paid and the principal and interest due on the Real Estate Contract, as well.

Since the seller/owner's name is still on the wrapped mortgage, it is the seller/owner's responsibility to notify the Escrow Agent if there is a change in the amount due on the prior obligations.

As a final note, in all situations wherein the mortgage is assumed or wrapped, it is necessary to make certain that the amount for taxes and insurance stated in the Real Estate Contract is the same as stated in the existing mortgage.

Terry Tip:
Having just recommended that an Escrow Agent be used in wrapped mortgage situations, I want to offer the following information. Let's assume a seller/owner has a 100-acre parcel of land that has been subdivided into two-acre lots, for example. A buyer/borrower could purchase one of those lots under a Real Estate Contract.

In this instance, the buyer/borrower's Contract payment would not be enough to cover the underlying mortgage payment of the 100-acre parcel. The buyer/borrower would be required to send the payment directly to the seller/owner, since Escrow Agents do not handle partial payments.

Further, the buyer/borrower would need to rely on the seller/owner to make the payments, as well as the difference, to the underlying mortgage. This would continue until such time as the requisite number of lots were sold to pay the underlying mortgage, and an Escrow Agent could be employed to receive and disburse the payments.

In a situation of this type, the buyer/borrower may want a lot-release clause incorporated into the Real Estate Contract to ensure that the buyer/borrower could obtain the warranty deed when one made the final payment on the Real Estate Contract. In addition, the buyer/borrower may want an annual verification document from the seller/owner that the mortgage on the 100-acre parcel is in good standing.

In the next chapter, we cover additional provisions that are included in a Real Estate Contract.

CHAPTER 12

OTHER PROVISIONS IN THE REAL ESTATE CONTRACT

There are several additional provisions to include in the Real Estate Contract and we discuss them here.

DUE ON SALE DISCLAIMER

If, in fact, the Real Estate Contract includes a wrapped mortgage, the Contract should include a disclaimer regarding the "due on sale" clause. It may be recalled that the due on sale clause was discussed in Chapter 7. In effect, the due on sale clause allows the mortgage lender to call the loan with an immediate pay-off of the outstanding loan balance, if the property is sold. In the Real Estate Contract the buyer/borrower is put on notice that the immediate pay-off of the mortgage is entirely the buyer/borrower's responsibility.

If the buyer/borrower on the Real Estate Contract does not comply, the Contract goes into default. If the default is not cured or corrected, the seller/owner may get one's property back with the balance on the mortgage due and payable immediately, which would then be the seller/owner's problem.

This disclaimer should be placed rather prominently in the Real Estate Contract. Both parties to the Contract should take

Chapter 12

heed and analyze the impact of this provision, in case the mortgage lender does call or accelerate the loan balance. Both parties should design an exit strategy in case this contingency occurs. My recommendation is that neither party should enter into the Contract without having assessed one's options in case the mortgage is called.

In Chapter 14, I provide an in-depth review of some possible problems or issues with wraps.

BUYER/BORROWER'S RIGHT TO SELL THE CONTRACT

Generally, there is a provision that discusses the buyer/borrower's right to transfer the Real Estate Contract. The provision outlines whether the buyer/borrower needs to obtain the seller/owner's consent before selling or assigning the property in the Real Estate Contract.

If no prior consent is required, the Contract is freely assumable and the buyer/borrower may sell, assign, convey, or encumber the property without the seller/owner's consent. Generally speaking however, the buyer/borrower is still obligated under the Contract unless written evidence of the transfer is provided to the Escrow Agent.

Even if the Real Estate Contract is freely assumable, if an assumed mortgage is part of the Contract, the buyer/borrower will want to ensure that the transfer of the Real Estate Contract does not run afoul of any provision in the assumed mortgage. Remember, the assumed mortgage is an addendum to the Real Estate Contract and if payments are not made on the assumed mortgage, this could trigger a default on the Contract.

Generally speaking, the buyer/borrower may transfer the Contract without paying off the balance of the Contract, if the buyer/borrower obtains the seller/owner's written consent to do so. If the seller/owner's written consent is required for the buyer/borrower to effect a transfer, and the buyer/borrower ignores this provision, the Contract may go into default. Moreover, the demand letter to cure the default may generally request the entire balance due the seller/owner at that time.

DEFAULT CLAUSE

The default clause gives recourse to the seller/owner in case the buyer/borrower does not adhere to the Real Estate Contract's terms. A default may be caused by the buyer/borrower missing a payment; not paying property taxes when due; not obtaining the required hazard insurance or public liability insurance; not making payments under an assumed mortgage; or by selling or transferring the Real Estate Contract without receiving prior written approval from the seller/owner, if applicable.

When default occurs, the seller/owner directs one's attorney to send what is called a *demand* letter that outlines the default, and stipulates the number of days the buyer/borrower has to *cure* or correct the default. If the default is not cured, the property generally is returned to the seller/owner. Note that this demand letter is an attempt to collect on a note, and as such is subject to the terms of the Fair Debt Collection Practices Act.

The number of days to cure the default is typically 30 days, but 60 days and even 90 days are used. Again, it is the number to which both parties agree and should be reviewed by an attorney. Note, as part of the Real Estate Contract, the buyer/borrower is obligated to pay the attorney's fee incurred in the drafting and mailing of this demand letter. The dollar amount of the attorney's fee for this letter is also stated in the Real Estate Contract.

If the default is not cured in the stated time, generally, the seller/owner presents the Escrow Agent with an Affidavit of Default, obtains the Special Warranty Deed from the Escrow Agent, and has the Special Warranty Deed recorded at the County Clerk's Office. The seller/owner now has title to the property.

Other issues may occur during the default process and things may not run as smoothly as described. In Chapter 13, I cover the default clause and process in detail.

MAINTENANCE

The insertion of this provision in a Real Estate Contract is a relatively recent development. The buyer/borrower is tasked with maintaining the property in the same good condition as it was when the buyer/borrower received it. This includes obeying any laws that cover the property, both structurally and environmentally.

Terry Tip:
I have been the seller/owner under many Real Estate Contracts, and I am pleased to see the maintenance provision become a standard in the Contract.

Generally, it has been my experience that when a Contract goes into default and the property is returned to the seller/owner, the buyer/borrower leaves the property in a state of damage and disrepair. I recall one instance in which the floor of a house that was returned to me was covered in six inches of garbage; and this was in every room. This is not always the case, however. In another instance of default, I discovered that the buyer/borrower had vacuumed the carpet before leaving!

Since it is impossible to predict the state of the property, this is one of the reasons I generally try to obtain a substantial down payment on the property. In case of default, I know there will be enough money to make the needed repairs and allow me to place the house back on the market.

ESCROW AGENT AND FEES

The Real Estate Contract lists the information for the designated Escrow Agent, as well as the party who will pay the fees for the account. Note, the fees can be split between both parties or the seller/owner may require the buyer/borrower to pay all of the fees.

Each escrow company has their various other fees for different services, but generally speaking there is a fee for setting up the escrow account, a disbursement fee, a close-out fee, and a fee for assignment in those situations wherein the seller/owner sells one's interest in the Contract or the buyer/borrower sells one's interest in the property. There is also a fee to transfer the escrow account to another company.

BUYER'S FINANCIAL QUALIFICATIONS

Another provision that may be inserted in the Contract is the seller/owner's right to approve the financial qualifications of the buyer/borrower. The seller/owner may call for a buyer/borrower's complete financial statement to include monthly income, verification of employment, debt to income ratio, and any other items, such as a credit report.

The seller/owner has the right to review this information and is given a period of time to conduct this review and accept or reject the application of the buyer/borrower. If the seller/owner does not conduct the review in the stated time period, it is assumed that the seller/owner rejects the buyer/borrower. In either case, outright declination or declination by default, the Real Estate Contract terminates and the seller/owner refunds the earnest money to the buyer/borrower.

As a point of information, there seem to be some requirements under the Dodd Frank Wall Street Reform and Consumer Protection Act that could require a seller/owner to document a buyer/borrower's ability to pay a Real Estate Contract. Questions about this and a seller/owner's specific situation should be directed to one's attorney.

In the next chapter, we cover the default process of the Real Estate Contract.

CHAPTER 13

DEFAULT PROCESS AND THE DEMAND LETTER

A default occurs when the buyer/borrower does not adhere to the terms of the Real Estate Contract.

Although generally a default is triggered by a missed payment, a default also may be caused by the buyer/borrower not paying property taxes when due, not obtaining the required hazard insurance or public liability insurance, not making payments under an assumed mortgage, or if applicable, by selling or transferring the Real Estate Contract without receiving prior written approval from the seller/owner.

The Real Estate Contract's default clause gives the seller/owner recourse in this case and starts the process and the timeframe whereby the buyer/borrower may cure (or rectify) the default. Note that there is no set number of times a Contract may go into default, providing the default is cured each time.

There are two remedies for the seller/owner to pursue if the buyer/borrower defaults and the default is not cured: the seller/owner may accelerate payment of the balance on the loan or the seller/owner may rescind the Contract and take back the property. In the latter option, the buyer/borrower forfeits the down payment and any scheduled payments already made to date.

The rescission of the Contract is the more popular of the two remedies and may be why some believe that a Real Estate Contract is good for the seller, but bad for the buyer. I think it is safe to state that generally when a seller/owner enters into a Contract with a buyer/borrower, the desire of both parties is to carry the Contract to completion.

The default clause is the main feature that makes a Real Estate Contract different from a Promissory Note and Mortgage, and a Deed of Trust.

THE DEMAND LETTER

Let's assume a situation of a missed payment wherein the payment on a Real Estate Contract is due on the 6th of the month. If the seller/owner does not receive payment on the 6th, the seller/owner may instruct one's attorney to send a demand letter to the buyer/borrower on the 7th.

This letter advises the buyer/borrower to cure the default in a stated time period. The cure default time period has been defined already in the Real Estate Contract that was signed by both parties. Generally, the timeframe is a 30-day period, but it can be as long as 60 days or 90 days, or even longer.

The demand letter is sent to the property address of record for the buyer/borrower, as listed in the Real Estate Contract. As stated in Chapter 8, if the buyer/borrower intends to rent the property that is the subject of the Real Estate Contract, an alternative "default" address should be given for the buyer/borrower and that should be shown in the Real Estate Contract.

The Contract generally requires the demand letter to be sent in two ways: certified mail with return receipt requested, and first-class mail. With a return receipt, the seller/owner may ascertain whether the buyer/borrower actually received the letter or declined to receive the letter. With first-class mail, if the letter is returned, it is generally stamped with the reason it is being returned and the reason may provide some indication of how to locate the buyer/borrower.

Usually, the Contract states that if a demand letter goes out, an attorney's fee may be collected from the buyer/borrower. Generally speaking, the seller/owner's attorney sends the demand letter; although, the seller/owner could compose and send the demand letter directly to the buyer/borrower. Since the wording of the demand letter is critical however, I strongly recommend engaging the services of a Real Estate Attorney for this function rather than the seller/owner trying to do it on one's own.

If the Real Estate Contract includes the provision that the buyer/borrower will pay the attorney's fee in connection with a demand letter, it also states the fee to be charged. Note, if the seller/owner writes the demand letter and sends it to the buyer/borrower, an attorney's fee may not be collected.

In addition to the buyer/borrower being mailed the demand letter, the Escrow Agent should also receive a copy of the demand letter. Unless the Escrow Agent is aware that there is a demand letter outstanding, it will not be in a position to know about or to collect the attorney's fee charged in connection with the demand letter.

Chapter 13

CONTENTS OF THE DEMAND LETTER

The demand letter must be clear and unambiguous in its wording. It is not a suggestion of what needs to be done, but a demand of what needs to occur for the buyer/borrower to cure the default.

The demand letter states the address of the property in question and the nature of the default; i.e., missed payment, lack of hazard insurance, etc. The letter outlines the details of what exactly needs to be done by the buyer/borrower in order to cure the default; by what date it is required to be done; and where it is required to be done, for example the Escrow Agent's office.

If the demand is not met within the cure default period, the letter advises that the seller/owner will either accelerate payment of the full balance of the loan or will rescind the Contract.

If there is a particular dollar amount to be delivered to the Escrow Agent, it should be stated. In the case of a missed payment, the amount of the payment is shown, as well as an amount for the attorney's fee for the demand letter, if applicable. As has been stated previously, an Escrow Agent is unable to accept anything less than the required amount that is due.

Let's assume a 30-day default period example. Rather than using the phrase of *within 30 days upon receiving this letter*, it may be better to state the exact date which is 30 days from the date the demand letter is mailed. This covers the contingency of the buyer/borrower not receiving the demand letter and avoids the question of when the 30-day count down begins. When a defined date is stated in the demand letter, there is no ambiguity; however, this could conflict with Federal Statutes, so I strongly recommend using an attorney.

If an attorney is sending the demand letter on behalf of the seller/owner, there is another provision that is covered in the demand letter regarding the Fair Debt Collection Practices Act (Act). This law was enacted by Congress in 1977 and is designed to prohibit debt collectors from using "abusive, unfair, or deceptive methods to collect" from consumers. According to this Act, the attorney who sends a demand letter on behalf of a seller/owner is considered a debt collector; the buyer/borrower is considered a consumer.

The Fair Debt Collection Practices Act provision in the demand letter advises the buyer/borrower of a certain action to be taken if the debt is disputed, and the timeframe in which to do this. If the buyer/borrower disputes the debt, the attorney must provide additional information. Note that this provision could impact the cure default date stated in the letter, and I recommend this aspect be discussed with an attorney.

THE REMEDIES

When the buyer/borrower cures the default, the seller/owner does not have to consider a remedy. The Real Estate Contract continues as if nothing had happened.

If the buyer/borrower does not cure the default, the seller/owner can then choose which remedy is appropriate for one's circumstances.

RESCISSION OF THE REAL ESTATE CONTRACT

Rescission of a Real Estate Contract is generally referred to as a non-judicial forfeiture. This means that the seller/owner is not generally required to go through the Court to have the property returned.

If the seller/owner elects rescission of the Real Estate Contract, the seller/owner may present an Affidavit of Default to the Escrow Agent. This Affidavit signifies an election to rescind the Real Estate Contract. The Affidavit states the parties to the Contract and provides the legal description of the property.

In addition, in the Affidavit of Default the seller/owner generally describes the steps taken to notify the buyer/borrower. If the seller/owner has the certified letter receipt, it is possible to show actual delivery of the letter. If the seller/owner does not have the certified letter receipt and has not had the first-class letter returned, it is presumed that the buyer/borrower received the demand letter. If the letter is returned or declined, these details are outlined in the Affidavit. The Affidavit of Default provides information that shows the seller/owner acted in good faith in notifying the buyer/borrower.

If the Escrow Agent determines that all is in order, the Special Warranty Deed is returned to the seller/owner, and the seller/owner should record it at the County Clerk's Office in the county in which the property is located. The seller/owner now has the right to take possession of the property.

When all goes well, the former buyer/borrower vacates the property willingly. If not, legal action may be taken by the seller/owner to have the former buyer/borrower removed.

During this time of legal action, the relationship changes into a landlord/tenant relationship and the seller/owner is able to collect rent while the former buyer/borrower occupies the property. Rent is due from the date the rescission is implemented. According to New Mexico law, the seller/owner/landlord may issue a written three-day eviction notice for non-payment of rent. Thereafter, the seller/owner/landlord may implement proceedings to have the buyer/borrower/tenant removed.

Terry Tip:
It has been my experience that sometimes these proceedings do not go as smoothly as one would hope. I had one experience wherein after purchasing an existing Real Estate Contract as an investment, the buyer/borrower did not make payments for six months.

After going through the demand letter procedure, I issued the three-day eviction notice and we went to Court. Now, with this particular Real Estate Contract, the buyer/borrower/tenant had made a substantial down payment of $20,000.00 on a $60,000.00 property.

At our first court hearing, the judge gave the tenant 90 days more in order to pay the rent that was owed. After 90 days, we appeared again; and this time, the buyer/borrower/tenant came to court with his baby who cried during the proceeding. The judge gave the tenant 90 more days to pay the rent that was owed.

After the second 90 days' period, we appeared in court again. This time the judge found in my favor and ordered the buyer/borrower/tenant to vacate the premises. At this point, the buyer/borrower/tenant had been living on the property for 12 months without making any payment.

As a point of information regarding this ruling, the judge advised the buyer/borrower/tenant that he could sue me for the down payment of $20,000.00 on the Real Estate Contract! This flies in the face of the intent of the Real Estate Contract, and the legal wording of the Real Estate Contract to which both parties (the seller/owner and buyer/borrower) had agreed. Experience has taught me that a judge can do whatever the judge wants to do.

Here we get into an area that I believe would be called "shocking the conscience of the Court." Although this phrase does not have a clear definition, it is sometimes used in Real Estate Contract situations wherein the Court changes the terms of the Real Estate Contract and the parties must abide by those new terms. If one engages in Real Estate Contracts, it is imperative to know about this phrase, and the impact it may have on transactions.

Regarding the foregoing story, the buyer/borrower/tenant did vacate the property, but not before totally trashing it by knocking holes in the walls, and stealing all the ceiling fans and some appliances. While making the repairs on this property so it could be put back on the market, I kept itemized receipts in case the buyer/borrower/tenant decided to sue me for the down payment. In effect, all of the $20,000.00 down payment went for repairs, and I was not sued.

BEWARE IF THE BUYER/BORROWER HAS A
FEDERAL TAX LIEN…

If the buyer/borrower has a federal tax lien attached to the property and the seller/owner elects to rescind the Contract, the seller/owner is obligated to notify the Internal Revenue Service (IRS) of the intention to rescind (Internal Revenue

Code Section 7425). In these circumstances, the termination or rescission of the Contract is defined as a "sale" by IRS.

According to Internal Revenue Code Section 7425, notification to the IRS must be done 25 days before the rescission is effected, and this can affect the date on which the seller/owner may want to implement rescission. Generally, the date of rescission is based upon the date on which the seller/owner presents the Affidavit of Default to the Escrow Agent. Due to this section's complexity, it would be wise to consult with one's attorney, should this situation arise.

In this IRS provision, there are certain requirements that attach to the way the notice must be made and the information required in the notice. This provision applies to any federal tax lien recorded at the County Clerk's Office more than 30 days before the date the seller/owner makes the election to rescind.

The IRS is given a redemption right of 120 days to determine whether it wants to buy the property. The 120 days are calculated based upon the date on which the seller/owner makes the decision to rescind the Real Estate Contract. In effect, the seller/owner is subsequently unable to sell the property during this 120-day period.

If the IRS makes the decision to redeem, the IRS buys the property for the sum of the seller/owner's unpaid principal balance, plus interest, to satisfy the federal tax lien. If the IRS does not redeem, the redemption right expires and the seller/owner may proceed with a subsequent sale.

The procedures outlined in Section 7425 of the Internal Revenue Code are critical for a seller/owner to understand,

and another reason for engaging the services of a Real Estate Attorney. The provisions in IRC Section 7425 state that if the notification procedure is not followed to the letter, the federal tax lien will survive the rescission of the Real Estate Contract, even if the 120-day redemption right terminates.

ACCELERATION

Instead of rescinding the Real Estate Contract, the seller/owner may accelerate payment of the unpaid principal balance, plus any accrued interest that is due on the Contract. To pursue this remedy, the seller/owner files a suit against the buyer/borrower for the balance due on the Contract.

In this situation, the seller/owner does not rescind the Contract. The buyer/borrower remains on the property, and the Escrow Agent maintains custody of the deeds. Through this remedy, it is assumed the Real Estate Contract will be paid in full and the buyer/borrower subsequently will obtain the deed and title to the property.

Although this is an option in the Real Estate Contract, it is infrequently used. There are several reasons that this may be the case; one of which is the fact that this option is costly because it involves litigation.

For the most part, generally, Real Estate Contracts go into default because of a missed payment. It is unlikely that a buyer/borrower would have the assets to cover the unpaid balance, if the reason for the default is that of a missed payment.

Ultimately, acceleration of the Contract may not be as economically efficient for the seller/owner as rescission is, especially in the instance wherein the property's value has been maintained or has appreciated. In rescission, the seller/owner is able to keep the down payment, as well as any scheduled payments that had been made to date. Subsequent to rescission, the seller/owner may sell what may be an appreciated property. This may be perceived as a better option for the seller/owner than simply receiving the unpaid principal balance, plus accrued interest on a property that had been valued at a lesser amount.

Terry Tip:
In all my years' experience, I have never seen this option elected, nor do I have first-hand experience. I have, however, heard of one instance in which this option was elected. According to the story I heard, when the seller/owner sued the buyer/borrower under the acceleration remedy, the judge on the case was alleged to have stated that since this was a Real Estate Contract the seller/owner should just rescind the Contract! Ultimately, I don't know the disposition of this case. I provide it for anecdotal purposes only.

SELLER/OWNER DEFAULT

Primarily, this chapter has dealt with the buyer/borrower defaulting on the Real Estate Contract. A question may arise regarding is there such a thing as a seller/owner default? And, if so, what are the remedies for the buyer/borrower?

Seller/owner default comprises areas such as refusing to convey title, failure to deposit the deed in escrow, failure to deliver title or provide title insurance, or misrepresentation of the property. Generally, the buyer/borrower must sue for remedy of the default.

CHAPTER 14

POTENTIAL ISSUES WHEN USING WRAPS

We have looked at Real Estate Contracts involving property that is owned free and clear, a first mortgage that is assumed, and a first mortgage that is wrapped. In this chapter, I discuss in detail some potential issues that may arise with a Wrap Real Estate Contract.

SETTING THE STAGE FOR THIS CHAPTER

When I teach my continuing education class on Real Estate Contracts, I routinely ask the question of those in attendance if they have heard the term "illegal wrap." It is not uncommon for some in the class to acknowledge that they have heard this term. This term may have come about because of the following scenarios.

There are some qualifying real estate brokers who will not allow their real estate professionals to buy or sell property under a Wrap Real Estate Contract. And, there are some who will allow it.

In addition, there are some title companies that will not close on a property that is bought or sold under a Wrap Real Estate Contract; and there are some that will.

Further, the title company that closes on a Wrap Real Estate Contract, as well as the attorney who draws up the Contract, may request the real estate professional and their qualifying broker to sign a hold-harmless agreement.

As an Escrow Agent with many years of experience, and as an individual who actively buys and sells property, I have seen Wrap Real Estate Contracts serviced; and I have entered into Wrap Real Estate Contracts.

As stated in Chapter 7, I personally do not have any problem with using a Wrap Real Estate Contract as long as both parties are knowledgeable regarding the provisions and possible consequences to using a Wrap Real Estate Contract.

That being said, I make the following disclaimer:

This author is not recommending or approving the use of a Wrap Real Estate Contract, but simply describing how a Wrap Real Estate Contract works. All parties involved must understand the complications involved with a Wrap and are strongly advised to seek legal counsel before entering into a Wrap Real Estate Contract.

A REVIEW OF THE WRAP REAL ESTATE CONTRACT

Before going into the potential issues involving a Wrap, I want to review the details of a Wrap Real Estate Contract. These details are excerpted from Chapter 7.

Using a Real Estate Contract with a wrapped mortgage is viewed as a way of trying to avoid the due on sale provision of an underlying mortgage. Mortgages with a due on sale clause allow the lender to call or accelerate full payment of the unpaid balance due on the mortgage, if the borrower sells or disposes of the property.

Chapter 14

With this scenario, the seller/owner has an outstanding mortgage that may not be assumed. The amount of the unpaid mortgage balance is added to the balance of the owner's equity in the property less the down payment, to achieve the Wrap Real Estate Contract's amount.

The buyer/borrower enters into the Contract with the seller/owner agreeing to make payments that will amortize the total amount of the Wrap Real Estate Contract. The seller/owner usually uses this payment to cover the underlying mortgage to the mortgage lender and agrees to maintain the mortgage in good standing.

The Wrap Real Estate Contract should be structured so that the term of the Contract is at least as long as the wrapped mortgage; and the payments are scheduled in such a way that allow the seller/owner's mortgage payment to be made in a timely manner.

The underlying mortgage remains in the seller/owner's name. The pay-off of the mortgage coincides with the pay-off of the Wrap Real Estate Contract; and the seller/owner agrees to turn over the deed to the buyer/borrower when the Wrap Real Estate Contract is paid in full.

Since the Wrap Real Estate Contract is executed to try to avoid the due on sale clause, the Contract may also contain a provision stating that the underlying mortgage may be called. If or when that happens, it is entirely the buyer/borrower's responsibility to make the payment of the total amount due. If the buyer/borrower fails to do so, it is considered as defaulting on the Real Estate Contract; and the cure default procedures are initiated.

IDENTIFYING THE ISSUES

The First Mortgage May Be Called

If the first mortgage is called, this is problematic for all parties.

The Buyer/Borrower's Dilemma

Although the Wrap Real Estate Contract can state that the buyer/borrower will be responsible to make a payment of the total amount due on the Contract if the first mortgage is called, how realistic is that? A good many buyer/borrowers enter into Real Estate Contracts in the first place, because they are unable to qualify for a mortgage.

If the first mortgage is called a short period of time after the Contract is executed, the buyer/borrower may not have had time to make the necessary changes to qualify for a loan. How will the buyer/borrower obtain the necessary cash to pay off the Contract?

If the buyer/borrower does not pay off the Contract, the Contract is in default and the seller/owner would be in a position to advise one's attorney to send a demand letter.

As a reminder, when the buyer/borrower does not cure the default, the buyer/borrower loses all the money invested in the property in the form of the down payment and monthly payments (if applicable) made thus far.

The Seller/Owner's Dilemma

Depending on the cure default period mentioned in the Contract, the seller/owner may be forced to wait at least 30 days or more before securing the property, and subsequently selling it (if the default is not cured) to obtain the cash needed to pay off the first mortgage.

If the seller/owner is unable to pay the principal balance on the first mortgage if it is called, the seller/owner may find oneself in a foreclosure situation. Not only could the seller/owner lose the property through foreclosure, the seller/owner's credit record would reflect a foreclosure.

The Mortgage Lender's Dilemma

The banks and mortgage lenders make money when they loan out money; they do not generally make money on properties on which they foreclose. Moreover, a bank or lender does not want to be in the real estate business; it does not want to own property or maintain property.

Is it logical to think that a bank or mortgage lender would call a loan that is being paid on time, if the bank or lender determined that the mortgage was part of a Wrap Real Estate Contract? I am of the opinion that if the mortgage is being paid on time, the bank or lender would not care about the wrap.

I believe this opinion may be supported by the backlog of foreclosures that accumulated during the recent housing-market crash. Some of the property that was foreclosed upon is still vacant and in need of repair.

It is true that the bank or mortgage lender would be within rights to exercise a due upon sale clause, but would that be in the bank's or mortgage lender's best interest if the payments were being made on time?

In my many years' experience as an Escrow Agent, I have never seen a bank or lender exercise the due on sale clause because of a Wrap Real Estate Contract. I have seen mortgages called for non-payment or other reasons.

Terry Tip:

Whenever I enter into a Wrap Real Estate Contract as either a buyer/borrower or a seller/owner, I analyze the situation and evaluate the contingency of the due on sale clause being exercised. I have a plan of action on which I have decided ahead of time and have made arrangements, in case this contingency occurs. Therefore, I am prepared in case the due on sale clause is exercised by the mortgage company.

Another Terry Tip:

As a final thought on the due on sale clause and for information purposes, I want to share a story from my experience. Several years ago, I received a call from one of our clients on whose Wrap Real Estate Contract our company was acting as Escrow Agent. He was agitated because the mortgage company was exercising its due on sale clause.

After ascertaining that his payments were being made on time, I advised him that in all my years' experience, I had never seen or heard of this happening. I suggested he call the mortgage company to see what his options were. Note that this is at a time when there were local mortgage companies and one could build a relationship with them.

Shortly thereafter, he called me back to say it had all been a mistake. He was a first-time homebuyer and as such, his mortgage contained the provision that he could not sell his property within the first two years of the mortgage. The mortgage company was under the impression that he was still within this two-year period when he sold the property, and that is why the loan was called.

Chapter 14

After the mortgage company determined that he was beyond the two-year period for first-time homebuyers, it rescinded exercising the due on sale clause. It did not have a problem with the mortgage being a part of the Wrap Real Estate Contract.

The Contract Payment May Be Late

As reviewed in the previous section, the payment for the Wrap Real Estate Contract is generally enough to pay the underlying mortgage and the seller/owner generally relies on that payment coming in to make the mortgage payment that is due.

If the seller/owner does not have the assets to cover the payment of the first mortgage, there could be consequences of late fees and adverse impact to the seller/owner's credit report if the Wrap Real Estate Contract payment comes in late. Recall that the mortgage stays in the name of the seller/owner in this scenario.

Since mortgages are generally due on the first of the month and late fees are generally incurred on the 16th of the month, setting the payment due date on the Wrap Real Estate Contract is critical. It is important to structure the payment due date on the Wrap Real Estate Contract so that the seller/owner will not be impacted by a late payment on the Wrap Real Estate Contract.

Let's look at a Wrap Real Estate Contract on which the payment is due on the 20th and the seller/owner relies on the Wrap Real Estate Contract payment to cover the underlying mortgage payment that is due.

Contract Payment Is On Time

Assuming 30-day months, if the Contract payment due date is on the 20th and the payment comes in on time, this allows the Escrow Agent or the seller/owner if an Escrow Agent is not employed, 10 days to ensure the mortgage payment reaches the mortgage company on the 1st.

Contract Payment is Late, Buyer/Borrower Cures the Default

If the Contract payment is late and does not come in on the 20th, the seller/owner may have one's attorney begin the cure default period by sending a demand letter. In the best case scenario, the seller/owner generally gives 30 days to cure the default.

If the buyer/borrower cures the default in 30 days by making a Contract payment, the seller/owner is able to make the mortgage payment, albeit late. The seller/owner picks up a late fee and this may be reflected on the seller/owner's credit report.

Chances are if the buyer/borrower cures the default, the buyer/borrower pays a late fee along with the Contract payment. Generally speaking, this does not have an adverse effect on the buyer/borrower's credit record.

Contract Payment is Late, Buyer/Borrower Defaults

For illustrative purposes, in this example we will use actual months of the year. If the buyer/borrower does not cure the default, the seller/owner is faced with taking back the property and selling it to another buyer/borrower after 30 days. In the scenario we are constructing with a Contract payment due date of June 20th, a cure default period would end on the 20th of July, the following month.

The mortgage payment due on July 1st is late, since the cure default period ends on July 20th. The seller/owner picks up a late fee on the mortgage payment on July 15th. If the seller/owner is unsuccessful in getting the property sold by August 1st which is the next month's mortgage payment due date, the seller/owner could be faced with two missed mortgage payments July 1st and August 1st, and possibly two late fees, depending upon when the property eventually sells.

In addition to the adverse impact on the seller/owner's credit report, the seller/owner may face foreclosure proceedings.

Terry Tip:
As the seller/owner of a Wrap Real Estate Contract, I recommend making one or two mortgage payments in advance of entering into a Wrap Real Estate Contract. In this way, the payments for the mortgage will always be one or two months ahead in case the buyer/borrower is late with a payment or defaults. The seller/owner will have a little more breathing room, before incurring late charges on the underlying mortgage and in selling the property in the case of default.

Note that it is always a good idea to check with the mortgage company after doing this to make certain that the mortgage payment is applied as desired, and not to principal reduction.

The Wrap Real Estate Contract May Pay Off Before the First Mortgage

The term of the Wrap Real Estate Contract should be structured so that it is at least as long as the wrapped mortgage; this is to ensure that the Wrap Real Estate

Contract does not pay off before the first mortgage. When the Wrapped Real Estate Contract pays off, the seller/owner is obligated contractually to turn over the deeds to the buyer/borrower.

Generally speaking, the payments and term of the Wrap Real Estate Contract should allow the Contract's principal balance to keep pace or gently lag with that of the underlying first mortgage.

If the Wrap Real Estate Contract pays off before the first mortgage, the seller/owner may be forced to pay off the underlying principal of the mortgage immediately to satisfy the terms of the Contract.

Buyer/Borrower Makes Unscheduled Payment

Remember, that scheduled payments on a Contract are worded in such a way that the buyer/borrower may pay the scheduled dollar amount, or more. Since the timing of the payoff of the Contract is critical, it is important that the proper Contract wording be used.

For example, let's say a buyer/borrower receives a large bonus at work or receives a sizeable tax refund and wants to apply it toward a Wrap Real Estate Contract. If the buyer/borrower does this, a situation may be created wherein the Contract pays off more quickly than the underlying first mortgage.

If we assume a $5,000.00 bonus or tax-refund amount remitted in addition to a $400.00 monthly payment, the following scenario may transpire.

The Contract may be worded that the $400.00 payment is applied to the underlying mortgage and any additional

132

payment is disbursed as the seller/owner directs. Generally, the extra payment is routed to the seller/owner, whether it goes directly to the seller/owner or through an Escrow Agent to the seller/owner.

It has been my experience as an Escrow Agent, that when the seller/owner receives an additional amount of money over what normally is expected on a Wrap Real Estate Contract, the seller/owner spends that additional amount of money. In the situation as described, the seller/owner should set aside this additional money to be used to pay off the underlying first mortgage rather than spend it.

When the additional money is remitted with the Contract payment, the balance on the Wrap Real Estate Contract is reduced. If the additional payment is not applied to the underlying mortgage, this could create a situation wherein the Wrap Real Estate Contract may pay off before the first mortgage. The seller/owner will be required to come up with an additional lump sum of cash in order to pay off the underlying first mortgage and deliver title to the buyer/borrower.

Terry Tip:
In order to avoid this happening, the Wrap Real Estate Contract should contain language that directs any principal reductions paid by the buyer/borrower to be applied to the underlying mortgage and not be paid to the seller/owner. This will ensure that the Wrap Real Estate Contract operates according to the way in which both parties expect.

Problems With Taxes and Insurance

Another area of the Wrap Real Estate Contract which may cause an issue is the provision dealing with taxes and insurance; and this generally has to do with an improperly drawn Contract.

In a Wrap Real Estate Contract, it is necessary to separate the payment for principal and interest on the Contract and to separate the payment for the taxes and insurance on the underlying mortgage. If the Wrap Real Estate Contract uses the seller/owner's monthly mortgage coupon amount that includes principal, interest, taxes, and insurance as the principal and interest payment for the Contract, this payment will be applied only to reduce the balance on the Real Estate Contract.

If this were to happen, it would create the situation seen in the previous section whereby the Wrap Real Estate Contract is paid off before the underlying mortgage.

Let's assume a $900.00 principal and interest payment on the underlying mortgage, and a $250.00 taxes and insurance payment. The total mortgage payment coupon amount is $1,150.00 and is applied as $900.00 to principal and interest, and $250.00 to taxes and insurance.

If the Wrap Real Estate Contract only identifies the payment as $1,150.00, the following may happen. The entire $1,150.00 is applied to the balance due on the Wrap Real Estate Contract, but the payment due on the underlying mortgage is separated appropriately and applied to principal, interest, taxes and insurance. This would create a situation wherein the Wrap Real Estate Contract could pay off before the underlying mortgage is paid off; and in effect, the seller/owner would be responsible for paying taxes and insurance.

Chapter 14

This may not be what the seller/owner desires, but once the parties agree on the wording of the Contract and sign it, the Contract is legally enforceable. That is why it is so important to obtain the services of a Real Estate Attorney when the Contract is drafted.

Equally important is the seller/owner's responsibility to advise the buyer/borrower or the Escrow Agent if applicable, of any increase in the payment of taxes and insurance.

Problems With Insurance

The insurance situation on a Wrap Real Estate Contract was covered in Chapter 11, and it is excerpted here.

There is not an easy answer of the way in which the insurance should be handled on a Wrap Real Estate Contract. As a point of information, there are three options that are discussed for insurance and they are presented.

Option 1:
The seller/owner maintains the original insurance policy on the property which is paid as a part of the monthly payment to the mortgage lender or mortgage servicer. The buyer/borrower obtains a homeowner's policy on the property according to the terms of the Wrap Real Estate Contract.

There is a possible issue here since in effect, the seller/owner is no longer the homeowner. In addition, there are two hazard insurance policies on the property. If there were a claim there would be two homeowners' policies. The insurance company for the seller/owner may say that it is the buyer/borrower's problem, and vice versa. Although this option has been used for many years, it appears this option may have some issues.

Option 2
The seller/owner makes the request of his property insurance agent to add the buyer/borrower as an additional insured on the seller/owner's original homeowner's policy. This may appear to the mortgage lender as a situation in which the buyer/borrower has loaned money to the original insured.

At issue here is that the seller/owner no longer owns the property, but is listed in the homeowner's policy as the homeowner. If there were a loss, the claim may not cover the buyer/borrower's belongings.

Further, in case of a loss, the claim proceeds check may be paid only to the seller/owner as the homeowner, or may be made payable to both of them. It would seem that both parties may have an issue with getting the insurance proceeds disbursed properly so that repairs could be made on the property.

Option 3
The seller/owner instructs the property insurance agent to change the homeowner's policy into a landlord's policy or a fire policy. The buyer/borrower would be instructed to obtain a renter's policy for the contents of the structure.

In this way, if there were a fire, the landlord's policy would cover the structure and the renter's policy would cover the contents of the structure. In effect, two separate claims would be made on two separate policies for two separate insureds.

In my research over the last several years regarding how the hazard insurance should be arranged on a Wrap Real Estate Contract, it has been the consensus of several property insurance agents that Option 3 is generally recommended.

Terry Tip:
When selling a piece of property with a wrapped mortgage, I recommend engaging the services of one's property insurance agent and explaining the terms of the Real Estate Contract to the agent, to see what the agent would recommend. After all, if there were a claim, it is the property insurance agent who will represent the seller/owner in the claim.

Summary

It is important that both the buyer/borrower and the seller/owner are knowledgeable regarding the potential risks involved with Wrap Real Estate Contracts. A problem can arise when individuals enter into Wrap Real Estate Contracts without knowing the ramifications or when Wrap Real Estate Contracts are not drawn up properly or worded correctly.

In the next chapter, I discuss the value of an Escrow Agent.

CHAPTER 15

ROLE OF THE ESCROW AGENT

In New Mexico, Escrow Agents are used as independent third parties in just about all Real Estate Contract situations. This has evolved over a period of years.

A BRIEF HISTORY

Before Escrow Agents began operations, banks, and savings and loan associations handled escrow activities for their clients and generally did not charge a fee for this. At that time, the number of Real Estate Contracts were few; and the Contracts were not complex.

With the advent of high interest rates, the number of Real Estate Contracts increased and became a little more complex, involving assumed mortgages and wrapped mortgages. Banks, and savings and loan associations began charging fees for their escrow activities. What had begun as a convenience for their clients became a burden to the banks and savings and loan associations.

Banks, and savings and loan associations found that their personnel were not equipped with the knowledge to handle these more complex Real Estate Contracts. Often mistakes were made that subjected the banks, and savings and loan associations to liability. This resulted in some of the organizations limiting the types of Real Estate Contracts that they would handle.

The increase in the number of Real Estate Contracts being executed spawned an industry of independent escrow companies formed solely for the purpose of servicing Real Estate Contracts, deeds of trust, and mortgages. These independent escrow companies were set up by individuals with legal, accounting, or real estate experience; they were knowledgeable about their industry and streamlined the processing of payments and the handling of accounts.

Some of the banks, and savings and loan associations began hiring these independent escrow companies to service the escrow accounts that they had in house. These independent escrow companies were unregulated at the time and some abuses occurred.

ESCROW AGENT REGULATION

In 1983, the Escrow Company Act was passed by the New Mexico Legislature and the independent escrow companies came under regulation.

Escrow Agents are regulated and licensed by the Financial Institutions Division of the New Mexico Regulation and Licensing Department. In this respect, Escrow Agents must pay for a license, reapply for a license every year, maintain a $100,000.00 bond, and follow the regulations applicable to Escrow companies.

An Escrow Agent must deposit any money coming into an escrow account into a separate trust account managed by a bank, a savings and loan institution, or a credit union located in New Mexico, prior to disbursing any money. The State of

New Mexico audits Escrow Agents about every 12 to 18 months or so to ensure that these trust accounts balance, and that the Escrow Agent's operations are in order.

If there is a complaint regarding the Escrow Agent's operations, it is filed with the Financial Institutions Division. The Financial Institutions Division forwards the complaint to the Escrow Agent requesting the Escrow Agent's side of the story. The Financial Institutions Division acts as intermediary between the two parties until the complaint is resolved.

ROLE OF THE ESCROW AGENT

In this book, we have discussed the role of an Escrow Agent as it pertains to Real Estate Contracts. As a neutral party, the Escrow Agent monitors the transactions under the Contract.

There are fees that must be paid to engage the services of an Escrow Agent; and generally these fees and to whom they will be charged, are outlined in the Real Estate Contract. There are no prescribed rules for the application of the fees; it is to whatever the parties of the Real Estate Contract agree.

To review, the Escrow Agent receives the monthly payments of the buyer/borrower and distributes them according to the terms of the Contract to the seller/owner and to the underlying mortgage, if applicable. The Escrow Agent calculates principal and interest, as well as the principal balance; and can hold money for taxes and insurance in an impound account to pay the taxes and insurance when due.

The Escrow Agent issues the Internal Revenue Service's Form 1098 Mortgage Interest Statement to the buyer/borrower that shows the amount of interest paid by the buyer/borrower on the Real Estate Contract. The seller/owner may obtain from the Escrow Agent a statement with the year-to-date principal and interest paid.

Escrow Agents hold the warranty deed and the special warranty deed for the subject property of the Real Estate Contract. When the Real Estate Contract is completed according to terms, the Escrow Agent releases the deeds to the buyer/borrower. If the Real Estate Contract is in default and the default is not cured, the Escrow Agent releases the deeds to the seller/owner after an Affidavit of Default is presented.

Note that the Escrow Agent does not need to be in the same county as the property, nor even in the same state as the property.

It is important to note that the role of the Escrow Agent is not limited solely to Real Estate Contracts, however. In addition to Real Estate Contracts, an Escrow Agent may administer personal loans, promissory notes, lease agreements, rentals, mortgages, and installment contracts.

REASONS TO USE AN ESCROW AGENT

As a point of information, individuals are not required to use an Escrow Agent to administer their Real Estate Contract. Aside from the fact that I am an Escrow Agent, it is my opinion that it just makes good business sense to hire professionals.

There is a reason why we hire professionals to perform services and that is because generally we don't know what we don't know. We are unable to ascertain possible problem areas or imagine where an issue may arise, until it has already happened. Generally speaking, hiring professionals from the outset results in less time, effort, and money being expended rather than hiring them after the fact.

An Escrow Agent administers the Real Estate Contract as a neutral third party and removes the burden of administration from the buyer/borrower and the seller/owner. The Escrow Agent keeps accurate records which may be accessed by both parties and sends out IRS Form 1098s reporting the interest paid on the loan to the buyer/borrowers.

Records

As the seller/owner, one should ask if it is worth the effort to try to keep one's records of the declining principal balance and interest payments by oneself; and ascertain what is involved. Would it be necessary to set up some sort of spreadsheet in order to do this?

Further, at the end of the year, the seller/owner would need to provide the buyer/borrower with a statement of principal payments and interest paid. What if the buyer/borrower who has also been keeping records arrives at a different amount? How will that be resolved? This could cause hard feelings between the two parties.

Escrow Agents have automated processes by which to keep track of the payments made and the interest paid. This certainly facilitates the process for all parties concerned. In addition, automation helps insure against inaccuracy.

Deeds

Then there is the issue of the deeds. If an Escrow Agent is holding the warranty deed and special warranty deed, there are procedures that must be followed before the Escrow Agent may release the deeds to either party. These procedures apply to a default that is not cured and/or the successful completion of the Real Estate Contract by the buyer/borrower.

If an Escrow Agent is not holding the deeds, who will? For example, if the seller/owner holds the deeds, what is to prevent the seller/owner from recording the deeds to take back the property unbeknownst to the buyer/borrower? If the buyer/borrower is unaware of this, the buyer/borrower could continue making payments for the property, and possibly end up with nothing to show for it, except legal proceedings.

Upon the buyer/borrower's successful completion of the Real Estate Contract, what happens if the seller/owner refuses to release the deeds as stated in the Contract? Again, we have a situation requiring legal proceedings in order to ensure that the Real Estate Contract operates according to its terms.

Assuming the buyer/borrower has control of the deeds, what is to prevent the buyer/borrower from taking the deeds and recording the warranty deed, thereby assuming title to the property that is subject to the Real Estate Contract? It may be necessary to employ legal proceedings in that situation for the seller/owner to regain title.

These "deed" situations all may be avoided by employing the services of an Escrow Agent.

Payments

An Escrow Agent administering a Real Estate Contract is aware of the amount of the payment that must come in monthly. While an Escrow Agent may accept more in the way of a payment, the Escrow Agent is not able to accept less. This establishes a safeguard so that the Real Estate Contract operates according to its terms.

Assumed Mortgage Contract with an Escrow Agent
When an Escrow Agent administers a Real Estate Contract with an assumed mortgage, the buyer/borrower sends in the total payment to the Escrow Agent. The Escrow Agent disburses the requisite amount to the underlying mortgage lender or servicer of the assumed mortgage. The balance of the payment is generally made to the seller/owner.

Once the seller/owner receives the payment from the Escrow Agent, the seller/owner is aware that the underlying assumed mortgage payment has been made. The seller/owner knows this, since the Escrow Agent is unable to accept a payment that is less than the monthly amount that is due according to the terms of the Real Estate Contract.

Assumed Mortgage Contract without an Escrow Agent
Contrast this with a Real Estate Contract that is not administered by an Escrow Agent, and instead the buyer/borrower sends the monthly payment for the assumed mortgage directly to the mortgage lender or servicer. In addition, in this scenario, the buyer/borrower sends the payment for the principal and interest for the Real Estate Contract directly to the seller/owner.

When the seller/owner receives the principal and interest payment for the Real Estate Contract, the seller/owner may assume that the Real Estate Contract is operating according to terms. But, what if the buyer/borrower sends only the payment to the seller/owner and does not send a payment to the mortgage lender or servicer for the underlying assumed mortgage?

In that situation, the seller/owner may not learn of the assumed mortgage payment not being made until the buyer/borrower receives a foreclosure notice from the mortgage lender or servicer. If the seller/owner had been aware, the seller/owner could have had one's attorney send a demand letter for the buyer/borrower to cure the default.

If the buyer/borrower did not cure the default, the seller/owner could have interceded and made payments on the assumed mortgage while working on obtaining the property during the default process. Without having adequate, current knowledge of the situation, the seller/owner is in a vulnerable position and may run chances of losing the property altogether.

WRAP Contract with an Escrow Agent
A similar, disadvantageous situation may be set up for the buyer/borrower with a Wrap Real Estate Contract wherein an Escrow Agent is not used. If an Escrow Agent is used with a Wrap Real Estate Contract, the buyer/borrower makes a total monthly payment to the Escrow Agent.

The Escrow Agent disburses that payment to the underlying mortgage, and to any additional charges for insurance that must be carried by the buyer/borrower. The balance of any payment that is not designated to reduce principal on the Wrap Real Estate Contract is disbursed to the seller/owner. The buyer/borrower knows that the Escrow Agent will make the disbursements according to the terms of the Wrap Real Estate Contract.

The seller/owner knows that since a payment has been disbursed, the Wrap Real Estate Contract is operating according to terms, and that the buyer/borrower has purchased the requisite insurance. The payment for the requisite insurance is part of the payment the Escrow Agent is expecting to receive; and the seller/owner knows that the Escrow Agent will not accept less than is due.

WRAP Contract without an Escrow Agent
Contrast this same scenario with one in which there is no Escrow Agent and the buyer/borrower sends the payment directly to the seller/owner. The buyer/borrower relies on the seller/owner to make the disbursement properly. The seller/owner could send the payment for the underlying mortgage to the mortgage lender or servicer and just pocket the rest.

In this way, the seller/owner could maintain one's credit since the mortgage is still in the seller/owner's name. The buyer/borrower would be unaware that the rest of the payment was not going to reduce the principal on the Wrap Real Estate Contract.

Conceivably, it is possible for this scenario to continue until the buyer/borrower requests a statement of principal and interest payments or until the buyer/borrower thinks the terms of the Wrap Real Estate Contract have been fulfilled. The buyer/borrower may not find out about this situation until approaching the seller/owner for the warranty deed, since in the buyer/borrower's mind, the Contract was fulfilled.

This scenario could most likely result in the buyer/borrower bringing legal proceedings against the seller/owner.

Taxes and Insurance

Then, there is the situation of the Real Estate Contract under which the subject property is owned free and clear by the seller/owner; the buyer/borrower has the property assessed for taxation in one's name. In these Real Estate Contract scenarios, the buyer/borrower generally purchases hazard insurance to cover the structure as the seller/owner's and buyer/borrower's interest may appear.

When an Escrow Agent is used, the buyer/borrower sends a payment to cover all of the obligations. The part of the payment that represents the principal and interest of the Real Estate Contract generally is disbursed to the seller/owner. The Escrow Agent then allocates the balance of the payment into an impound account to pay taxes and insurance when these bills come due.

Again, once the seller/owner receives a payment, the seller/owner knows that the Real Estate Contract is operating according to terms and the full payment was received. Taxes are paid and the property is insured.

When an Escrow Agent is not used, the buyer/borrower sends the payment for principal and interest directly to the seller/owner, and sends the payment for taxes and insurance directly to the County Assessor and the insurance company. As long as the seller/owner is receiving a payment, the assumption may be made that the County Assessor and the insurance company are receiving their payments. This may not be the case.

The buyer/borrower could forego payments for the taxes and insurance, and the seller/owner generally would not be aware of this until an incident occurred, such as a tax lien being issued or a default on the Real Estate Contract. Imagine the situation of a default not cured by the buyer/borrower in which the seller/owner obtained the property, but with a tax lien attached to it.

Imagine further the situation of a default which was not cured and the seller/owner obtained the property only to find it was now an empty lot. The structure had burned down and the buyer/borrower had not purchased the required hazard insurance. What once had been a Real Estate Contract for a $100,000.00 property for example, is now a lot worth $20,000.00.

Unless and until the seller/owner asks for proof that the required insurance has been obtained by the buyer/borrower for the Wrap Real Estate Contract, the seller/owner relies on the assumption that the buyer/borrower has done so.

SUMMARY

I am not suggesting that all individuals are inherently dishonest, nor am I suggesting that all individuals generally enter into Real Estate Contracts with the intent to deceive. The only thing I am suggesting is that these adverse situations could have been avoided had the parties to a Real Estate Contract used an Escrow Agent for the administration of the Contract.

CHOOSING AN ESCROW AGENT

The purpose of this chapter is to outline the importance of using an Escrow Agent to administer Real Estate Contracts to avoid costly mistakes and disputes. With the Escrow Agent as a neutral third party, the seller/owner and buyer/borrower can be certain that all transactions are processed according to the terms of the Real Estate Contract, with attention to detail and absence of bias.

I recommend finding an Escrow Agent with whom one enjoys working and in whom one trusts. As Escrow Agents, we all do the same thing. It is important for individuals to find a company with whom they like doing business.

In the last chapter, I want to discuss why Sunwest Escrow, LC is the Escrow Agent of choice.

CHAPTER 16

SUNWEST ESCROW, LC—ESCROW AGENT OF CHOICE

I hope this book has been helpful. I wrote this book as an informational guide for Real Estate Professionals and any other individuals who may be interested in Real Estate Contracts.

As I mentioned previously, Real Estate Contracts are not for everyone, but they do provide individuals who otherwise may not qualify, an opportunity to purchase real property. I recommend that Real Estate Professionals, as well as other individuals who have an interest, should be aware of a Contract's advantages and disadvantages, and how they operate. In addition, I advocate using a team of professionals before entering into any owner-financed arrangement.

Real Estate Contracts are an option. They are just one more tool in the toolbox. It was my intention to give a broad overview of owner financing, and Real Estate Contracts in particular. That was my desire. When all the parties to the Real Estate Contract are informed of what is required of them as a party to the Contract, the chances are likely that the Contract will operate smoothly.

I have stressed the importance of using an Escrow Agent in Real Estate Contract transactions. In my many years' experience as an Escrow Agent, I have seen the incidents that can befall parties who decide to go it alone. I reiterate that it just makes good business sense to use an Escrow Agent; and I hope that I have presented a convincing argument in the previous chapter to that effect.

Having said that, I invite anyone interested in the services of an Escrow Agent to take a look at Sunwest Escrow, LC. I am rather partial to that company and I would like to invite you to make it your Escrow Agent of choice.

HISTORY

The company began as a small escrow company in October 1987 with one employee; it was called First Financial Escrow. In the first 10 years of business, First Financial Escrow grew by accepting new accounts and by acquiring small escrow companies in the region. It established a reputation for being honest, hardworking, and fair.

In 1997, First Financial Escrow purchased all of the escrow accounts from Sunwest Bank and at that time, changed its name to Sunwest Escrow, LC. Through this purchase, the number of escrow accounts under management increased from 2,000 to 10,000.

As one of the shareholders at the time and based upon my financial services background, I wanted to expand the business into Self-Directed Individual Retirement Accounts (Self-Directed IRAs), as well. In 2003, Sunwest Trust was formed, and shortly thereafter the company was granted its trust powers from the State of New Mexico Financial Institutions Division.

We continued under the name of Sunwest Trust and in 2004 began work on developing the Self-Directed IRA business. We handled the escrow accounts under the name of Sunwest

Trust; and until recently, this made Sunwest Trust the only company in New Mexico with the ability to act as an escrow agent and as a custodian for Individual Retirement Accounts.

In January 2016, Sunwest Escrow, LC and Sunwest Trust, Inc. were split apart and now operate as two separate, privately-owned companies in Albuquerque, New Mexico. The two companies operate under the same roof in the Sunwest building.

The escrow arm of our business has been in operation since 1987, and we are still going strong. Since the first day of operations, we have been regulated by the State of New Mexico and routinely undergo audits by the state. Through our employees' hard work and dedicated service, as well as through our acquisitions, we have continued to grow.

PHILOSOPHY

We have earned a reputation of being honest, hardworking, and fair. Training and education are important components of these standards, not only for our employees, but for the company's clients, as well. We listened to our clients and learned how to become the type of company with whom they want to do business.

I believe that clients will be happier with their Sunwest experience when they have all the information at their disposal. We have worked to accomplish this. Our websites contain information and forms for both Sunwest Escrow and Sunwest Trust. Fee schedules for each company are easily accessible from these websites, as well as access to clients' respective accounts.

Our Sunwest employees are trained so that whomever answers the phone is able to respond to your question without having to transfer you to another person. Employees are empowered and encouraged to make decisions. As the CEO, I support this philosophy; and employees know that I will support them as long as they can demonstrate that the decision at which they arrived was based upon our four core values: integrity, compassion, reliability, and ownership.

Training does not stop once the employees have mastered their positions; there is ongoing training in successful business principles and life principles so that employees may become more well-rounded.

In regard to employees' health and well-being, the Sunwest building has a gym on site. Employees may go to the gym on their lunch hour to work out, or they may take advantage of the trainers that are on site five times per week. The trainers conduct classes at the end of the work day, and there are different levels of workouts offered so that all may benefit.

Both companies are also active partners in national and community affairs. Both companies donate a percentage of their profits each year to various charities; some are local charities and others are part of national organizations.

The focus of these charities is homelessness for adults and children, domestic violence, and veterans' health and well-being. Employees are encouraged to take an active part in volunteering for these charities. Often, employees volunteer as a group and donate their time on site at a local charity.

SERVICES

The accounts that Sunwest Escrow administers are not limited solely to Real Estate Contracts, however. In addition, Sunwest Escrow administers personal loans, promissory notes, lease agreements, rentals, mortgages, and installment contracts. We hold funds, deeds, or other instruments, as well as collect and distribute other payments. Sunwest Escrow provides third-party accounting which ensures accuracy, reliability, and proper administration.

There is a wealth of information on the Sunwest Escrow website, and access to service forms, as well as videos which address the subject of Real Estate Contracts from both the buyer/borrower's and seller/owner's point of view. The following are some of the services that Sunwest Escrow provides to the parties of a Real Estate Contract.

Escrow companies charge fees for their services. Generally, there is some type of set-up fee, disbursement fee, close-out fee, and assignment fee. As was mentioned in the previous chapter, the party who pays these fees is designated in the Real Estate Contract. The fees vary from company to company, and there is no set table of fees used in the industry. Sunwest Escrow posts its fees on the webpage.

At Sunwest Escrow, records are maintained by account number, and electronic access to the escrow account is provided through our website. Parties may obtain up-to-date information by accessing their account in this way or through an automated phone line.

For the buyer/borrower, Sunwest Escrow will provide payment coupons which they may use to mail, or drop by our office, to make payments. In addition, we are able to set up an automatic draft from the buyer/borrower's bank account to make the monthly payments.

Proper credit is given for each payment received. In those instances in which a bad check is received or we are advised of insufficient funds, Sunwest Escrow may advise the buyer/borrower that a certified check will be required for future payments. Generally speaking, payments received are sent to the mortgage servicing company within a 24-to-72 hour period.

Along with disbursing payments to the mortgage servicing company, Sunwest Escrow will make deposits of payments into the seller/owner's bank account, if that is what is desired. Otherwise, the payment will be mailed directly to the seller/owner at the address of record.

Sunwest Escrow offers the seller/owner the service of a *Seller Account Monitoring Service* which automatically advises the seller/owner's attorney of record to send out a demand letter. The letter is triggered when a payment is late, and the seller/owner specifies on which date of the month the demand letter is to be mailed.

As administrator of a Real Estate Contract, Sunwest Escrow will generally not make changes on the account unless the changes are requested in writing and signed by both parties. Note, that if the seller/owner wants to change the bank account into which payments are deposited, this change will not require the signature of both parties.

Sunwest Escrow will provide an amortization schedule for the account upon request; it will show the calculation based upon periodic interest. This shows 12, 30-day periods based upon a 360-day year.

If the schedule is requested for daily interest, it is an estimate only. As may be recalled, daily interest is based upon a 365-day year and is calculated from the date on which the payment is received until the next date on which the payment is received. The amortization schedule is an estimate since any change in the date on which the payment is received would alter the calculation.

Our company does not report a buyer/borrower's payment information to the Credit Bureau. We will provide the buyer/borrower a detailed payment history of the account that a buyer/borrower may use in lieu of a credit report, however.

When a seller/owner sells one's interest in the Contract, we will notify all parties that Sunwest Escrow has received an assignment of interest. This is important so that the buyer/borrower knows to whom to address questions.

As an interested party to a Real Estate Contract, if there are any concerns with the way in which Sunwest Escrow is handling the account, I strongly encourage clients to call directly to try to clear up the issue. As a business practice, I give out my personal phone number in case there is a problem, and invite clients to call me. This is how we do business.

I mentioned earlier that Sunwest Escrow has grown by acquiring other escrow companies. When Sunwest Escrow buys out another Escrow Agent, it is the practice for Sunwest Escrow to give 30-day notices to all buyers and sellers to decide whether they want to name another Escrow Agent or whether they want to stay with Sunwest Escrow.

Note that buyers and sellers have to agree on the Escrow Agent; it is not possible for the buyer/borrower to have one Escrow Agent and the seller/owner to have a different Escrow Agent. If they don't name another Escrow Agent, Sunwest Escrow keeps the account and sends out coupons.

Finally, I am a firm believer in the phrase that knowledge is power. This is one of the reasons I teach continuing education classes on the subject of Real Estate Contracts, from a basics perspective to an advanced perspective. Real Estate Professionals are the target audience, but when there is room, I open up the class. The classes are presented from an Escrow Agent's point of view and are designed to identify problem areas before they are encountered.

SUMMARY

I am proud of our companies and our employees, and what we have accomplished. We have a dedicated group of people who enjoy what they do, and want to make the Sunwest Escrow experience a pleasure for all of our clients.

If you have a client who is considering entering into a Real Estate Contract; or you are considering entering into a Real Estate Contract; or you already have a Real Estate Contract administered by another Escrow Agent and do not feel you are getting the service that you want or deserve; please consider Sunwest Escrow as your Escrow Agent of Choice.

SUNWEST ESCROW, LC
10600 MENAUL BLVD. NE
ALBUQUERQUE, NEW MEXICO 87112
PHONE: 505.237.2225
FAX: 505.275.1554
TOLL-FREE: 1.800.642.7167
WEBSITE: www.sunwestescrow.com
EMAIL: tlw@sunwestescrow.com

Made in the USA
San Bernardino, CA
06 January 2017